Printed in the United States of America
First Printing, 2016

ISBN 978-0-9882727-1-2

Library of Congress Number: 2015921373

US Copyright (Pending) 1-2996937811

2225 Mundare Drive
Henderson, NV 89002

www.discoverAegis.com
info@discoverAegis.com

Ordering Information:
Quantity sales. Special discounts are available on quantity purchases by wholesalers, corporations, associations, and others. For details, contact the publisher at the email address above.

Disclaimer:
This book is presented solely for educational and personal development purposes. The author and publisher are not offering it as legal, accounting, or other professional services advice. While best efforts have been used in preparing this book, the author and publisher make no representations or warranties of any kind and assume no liabilities of any kind with respect to the accuracy or completeness of the contents and specifically disclaim any implied warranties of merchantability or fitness of use for a particular purpose. Neither the author nor the publisher shall be held liable or responsible to any person or entity with respect to any loss or incidental or consequential damages caused, or alleged to have been caused, directly or indirectly, by the information or programs contained herein. No warranty may be created or extended by sales representatives or written sales materials. Every company is different, and the advice and strategies contained herein may not be suitable for your situation. You should seek the services of a competent professional before beginning any improvement program. The story and its characters and entities are fictional. Any likeness to actual persons, either living or dead, is strictly coincidental.

*A*cknowledgements

"God has blessed me with a family who is deeply unimpressed by me."
Patrick Lencioni

My unyielding thanks and appreciation to Lynn Jacquart for showing up at the perfect time. I love you. I will always love you and I look forward to our life together.

Thank you to my family for their continued support and tolerance. Thanks for reminding me daily that I am not a big deal. And yes, the trash is at the curb. I am immensely proud of you Matt and Chris.

Great thanks to my team members who consistently support my efforts and work tirelessly to make me look good. Or as good as I can.

Hope you are proud mom and dad. Dad hope you approve of this work. You gave me your work ethic, tenacity, and stubborn determination to pursue my dreams and passion.

A final thank you to Sydney Marie for not caring who I am, what I am or what kind of day I had. You have been a great constant over the past nine years, and you are my spirit dog.

Contents

Introduction

I am the dad and primary caregiver to three dogs: two corgis, Sammy and Sydney, and a dachshund named Sadie. Throughout my childhood and my adult life, I have immensely enjoyed the company of dogs.

When I spend time engaging my dogs, listening to them, and consistently meeting their needs in a kind and meaningful way, they are more functional and much more likely to do what I want them to do. Conversely, when I leave them to their own wits for extended periods of time, they get into trouble. They dig. They eat couches. They fight. They poop in the hallway.

My human children behaved in the same manner. When I worked hard to make a healthy environment for them, they were much more likely to do what I wanted and much less likely to voice resistance.

And so it is with our employees and team members.

Enough about My Dogs and Kids

In over twenty years as a leadership and organizational development consultant, I have seen some very healthy organizations. They were open, their leaders were people centric, they were ethical, they solicited input, and they produced exceptional results. Unfortunately, I have also witnessed quite a few unhealthy organizations which, try as they may, just can't get their act together. And their bottom line shows it.

For my purpose, the lessons learned from both healthy and unhealthy organizations have equal value. We learn greatly from the actions and inactions of both models.

If you are hoping to read this book and find a single magical answer to transform your organization from a state of dysfunction to a state of health, I am truly sorry. You will not find that here. Rather, you will find a series of steps, practices, and actions that can help you breathe real life into your company.

Employee Engagement is Not Enough

This is not a book about employee engagement. There is far more to organizational health than just engagement. Because engagement has developed some significant stigmas over the past few years, team members now look at engagement as nothing more than an exercise in completing a survey. In their eyes, a survey does not produce relevant changes and contains dubious levels of confidentiality. While I am not saying this adequately defines engagement, many team members view it with skepticism.

Similarly, managers also look at engagement as an exercise. Many have a competitive fervor that is shown in how they compare data with fellow managers, and they are crestfallen when their results are not as expected. An additional disturbing trend is the amount of time managers spend in debunking certain comments or parsing the data provided by the engagement reports. Inordinate amounts of time are wasted showing the issue is located only within the graveyard shift and not within the entire department. Really?

Who cares? Why are managers trying so hard to deflect indicators of poor levels of engagement?

If, like me, you have ever read the news capsules of companies that win local, regional, and national "best places to work" awards, some of them sound like country clubs. Those companies and organizations tout workout rooms, flexible scheduling, coffee bars, and Friday massages. Those corporations are clearly focusing on team member satisfaction and engagement but not on overall health. By enticing workers with material objects and superficial perks, the engagement trap is set.

This is a trap because, although needs are being met, those needs are superficial and potentially short-lived. In 1901, Ivan Pavlov and Ivan Filippovitch Tolochinov proved people will respond to conditional reflex. [1][2] They further proved that when the rewards diminished, the responses slowed and stopped. If budget restrictions force the cancellation of Friday massages, what do you have now? Do your team members begin looking for the best engagement related benefits from other employers? Can the removal or neglect of an engagement strategy create disengagement?

Nevertheless, engagement strategies will be a big part of driving organizational health. A great deal of the research for this book was related to engagement strategies and the effect they have on overall success. Team member engagement is an important ingredient for organizational health, but only when it is administered and delivered in a holistic and global manner.

For our purposes, team member engagement will be defined as a series of processes and actions designed to create enthusiastic team members who desire arriving at their workplace. Simply stated, an engaged team member is one who wants to be at work. That is not to say they wouldn't quit if they won the lottery, but they enjoy coming to work; work provides several key satisfaction and need points for your team members.

Organizational Health is Not Enough

It becomes almost counter-intuitive that a book devoted to organizational health proclaims that organizational health is not enough to be successful.

But it isn't enough.

Successful organizations must have three other components in play to be truly successful. Operational excellence, market and product, and direction and culture must be present along with organizational health in order to create success. Ultimately, without all four working together in near equal proportions, no organization will be successful in a long and sustained manner.

Operational excellence is the group of actions required to produce and deliver your product or service. This includes your staffing level or right sizing, your procedures for product and service delivery, and your efficiency and effectiveness in your operation. All cylinders are firing in a manner needed to deliver product. Please note that in the sentence above, the term *procedure* was used and not the term *policy*. This is a big difference and one that will be discussed later in relation to input and voice.

Market and product refer to the overall value, quality, and desirability of your product. Also included is the approach you have in engaging customers and potential customers. This incorporates marketing, advertising, brand identity, and quality.

The final component of successful organizations is direction and culture. This includes vision, mission, culture, and values prescribed by a company. Of equal importance is the consistent commitment and dedication to those directional elements.

Moving Towards Organizational Health

So why focus on organizational health?

Out of the four key areas for organizational success, health becomes the one that can be positively influenced the most quickly and produce the most sustained impact. It is also the area of success that can be driven on both a micro level and a macro level in an organization. This means that companies can certainly embrace and drive organizational health but so can individual departments, divisions, and operating units.

Beyond engagement and creating an environment in which team members want to come to work, healthy organizations provide meaningful formal and informal systems to provide team members with voice and input. Separate from engagement strategies, these processes also have a significant impact on enhancing team member effort through buy-in and producing much higher levels of innovation and creativity.

We will also explore the role of talent management, people focused leadership practices, service-based culture, transparency, and ethical congruence to complete the ingredient list for a healthy organization. But more importantly than that, we will also use some current research to answer the question of why any of this matters. Here is a hint; it matters, and it matters big.

Please enjoy this view of healthy organizations and how to get there. Your feedback is always appreciated.

Chapter 1

Why It Matters

"The best morale exist when you never hear the word mentioned. When you hear a lot of talk about it, it's usually lousy."
Dwight D. Eisenhower

Answering the why is both pretty simple and a bit convoluted at the same time.

Repeat this mantra over and over again: "Happy team members work harder, produce quality, and deliver great service." There it is in a nutshell. Why this whole thing matters.

Simple in that, since December 1990 when William Kahn published his groundbreaking work, *Psychological Conditions of Personal Engagement and Disengagement at Work*, there have been a huge number of studies related to the impact of engagement and healthy workplaces.

The convoluted and difficult part comes from differing definitions of engagement and organizational health cited in many studies. For our part, we will focus on the most straightforward research available.

First, let's get one thing straight. A healthy working environment and moving beyond engagement is not about all of the touchy, feely, makes them happy stuff. A healthy working environment is about results: sustained results. There is no other reason to work on these strategies.

In 2012, Gallup conducted the most cited and comprehensive study of its kind focusing on team member engagement and the impact engagement has on key results and success factors including customer service, turnover, productivity and profitability. *Engagement At Work: Its Effect On Performance Continues In Tough Economic Times* uses a sampling size of 1.4 million team members in 192 business

units spanning all industry and size segments.

Their most indicative and important finds included this:

> 37% lower absenteeism, 25% lower turnover (in high-turnover organizations), 65% lower turnover (in low-turnover organizations), 28% less shrinkage, 48% fewer safety incidents, 41% fewer quality incidents (defects), 10% higher customer metrics, 21% higher productivity, 22% higher profitability

So, let me summarize a bit here: everything you value

and need to have happen in your organization can be improved

and enhanced when you utilize a series of engagement

strategies. The Gallup people said it best in their report:

> The concept of employee engagement has become a common idea in the business world, as many studies have demonstrated its importance to organizational performance and shown how companies can measure and act on it. Many large-scale studies started in the late 1990s have demonstrated that business units with more engaged employees have better odds of achieving the outcomes their organizations desire such as revenue, profit, customer engagement, safety, quality work, and employee retention.

In Employee Engagement: Maximizing Organizational

Performance, Right Management Consultants, a Manpower

Company, summarizes their findings on engagement by saying:

Engaged employees are 7 times less likely to leave in the next year and 1.5 times more likely to stay for at least 5 years. Organizations need to protect their investments in their workforce by retaining employees and their intellectual capital to ensure business continuity and the ability to meet key business objectives. Does your organization know who is engaged and who isn't? This can be the best starting point for addressing unwanted attrition that could lead to competitive weakness should your top performers leave.

Engaged employees lead to increased productivity, retention, customer loyalty and profitability.

Measurement without action can do more harm than good. Simply surveying for the current engagement level and then doing nothing with that information often leads to employees feeling that they aren't being heard, which in turn can negatively impact morale and trust levels.

Likewise, the other primary factors associated with organizational health; ethical congruence, transparency, input and voice, service culture, and people focused leadership have similar, if a bit less documented, impact on results. When you combine all the factors, you are well on the way to building a high-performance working environment.

Without going full-blown research thesis mode on you, the evidence is clear and compelling. Engagement strategies and healthy organization strategies work and provide a solid return on investment.

So, if increased profit, higher productivity, lower turnover, and greater service levels matter, you will begin the process of building a healthy organization.

Chapter 2

𝒯alent Management as a Healthy Organization Driver

"You can tell the ideals of a nation by its advertisements."
Norman Douglas, South Wind

You are no better than the people you hire and retain in your organization. Your regrets may be built on the people that have left you or the ones you were unable to hire.

Very clearly, Jim Collins in his iconic work *Good to Great* said:

> *"Get the right people on the bus, the wrong people off the bus, and the right people in the right seats."*

> *"For no matter what we achieve, if we don't spend the vast majority of our time with people we love and respect, we cannot possibly have a great life. But if we spend the vast majority of our time with*

*people we love and respect – people we really
enjoy being on the bus with and who will never
disappoint us – then we will almost certainly have
a great life, no matter where the bus goes. The
people we interviewed from the good-to-great
companies clearly loved what they did, largely
because they loved who they did it with."*

*"The moment you feel the need to tightly manage
someone, you've made a hiring mistake. The best
people don't need to be managed. Guided,
taught, led–yes. But not tightly managed."*

Mr. Collins understood the role of talent management in
the overall achievement of a healthy and high-performing
organization.

This section will not tackle the entirety of the complex
world of talent management but will really focus on one aspect:
who we hire and how we find them.   In this regard, talent
management becomes an incredibly important part of overall
organizational health. If you are not recruiting and retaining
candidates that respond to healthy organization initiatives, your
efforts will be for naught.

The litmus question that I have asked leaders for over two decades revolves around identifying the problem team members. Think for a moment about the thick-file team members who have consistently been on and off of document disciplinary actions, those who have filed grievances, those who have complained about you.

Are those team members difficult and problematic because of a lack of technical skills? Are they problematic because of a lack of educational level? Or is it something entirely different such as poor attitudes, poor fit within the culture, or poor interpersonal skills?

If you, like the vast plurality of those I ask, indicated they are problematic team members because of poor attitudes, poor cultural fit, or because of a lack of interpersonal skills, we will then progress on through the talent management conundrum involved.

Now look at your job advertisements, internal job announcements, and position descriptions. What do you see now? Do these highlight technical skills and education levels, or do they look closely at desired attitudes and interpersonal skills such as communication, customer service, teamwork, emotional intelligence, and conflict resolution? Now you see the conundrum involved.

You Catch What You Go Fishing For

My dad was not a particularly well-educated man (high school graduate but only to play basketball) (last in a class of eight) but he told me once that you catch what you go fishing for. And he was right. If your job bait is looking for a certain educational level or number of years of experience, then that is exactly what you will catch. And then we feign surprise when it turns out they don't have the interpersonal skills needed to be successful, and they actually become a toxic team member that has an adverse effect on organizational health and team engagement.

As it relates to talent management, the solution here is clear. In all job advertisements and announcements, highlight the needed communication, teamwork, and other interpersonal skills that relate directly to organizational health. Talk about your culture and how a team member's positive attitude is highly desirable. Use words like upbeat, motivated, engaged, involved, communicative, positive, and connected to describe a desired team member. Avoid any overemphasis on experience or education level.

Consider some of these examples:

> Fast paced and very customer focused environmental engineering firm is seeking a professional engineer that works well with others, communicates effectively, and provides exceptional levels of customer service. Experience in infrastructure projects and PE certification is desirable but fit with our existing team is more important than all other factors.

> OR

> An internationally recognized five-star integrated resort is interested in adding a technology architect for our information and data department. This individual must demonstrate positivity, ability to work with others, commitment to stakeholder needs, and the desire to communicate constantly with key stakeholders. We are not interested in a run-of-the-mill candidate and will only consider those people who are exceptional supporters of our culture and values.

OR

If you enjoy interacting with customers and fellow team members, consistently maintain and display a positive attitude and work flexibly through a variety of issues, our automobile service company has a career path for you. We will provide an excellent working environment in return for your great efforts and ability to work within our system.

Interview and Test with an Eye on Organizational Health

No job interview should be a recap of someone's resume' or application. In fact, the items listed on those documents should be rarely discussed or referenced.

To make a dent in overall organizational health, leaders and talent managers must use behavioral interview questions related directly to those behaviors desired for a healthy environment. You will want to test for communication desire, ability to work well with others, willingness to provide internal and external service, skills associated with working through difficult and changing situations, and problem-solving competencies.

You also want to get the pulse of a job candidate's attitude. This can be a little slippery at times, but it is doable and must be done. Do you want consistent upbeat and engaged team members or do you want another of your thick-file team members?

In an age of extremely well-prepared job applicants, throwing a curve in a behavioral interview is more difficult. Consider using some of the following questions to connect a candidate's skills to your desired outcomes in organizational health:

> Describe how you would work with and diffuse a difficult customer.
>
> Talk about how you have worked successfully with difficult or challenging co-workers.
>
> Tell me what kind of things you do to ensure a high level of internal service to other departments and fellow team members.
>
> Describe your desired approach to communication during a project.
>
> What are the things that you do to work well with others?
>
> How do you build consensus among team members or when competing deadlines exist?

How do you manage your own attitude and approach?

Describe, in some detail, your demeanor under pressure and when deadlines and customer demands are looming.

How do you react and respond when priorities change or when you have to manage multiple priorities?

How do you stay upbeat and positive when times are challenging?

When faced with a difficult co-worker, please describe your approach to working with them.

This is not an all-inclusive list but rather a set of examples that you can use to build your own questions. In each of the examples above, as well as behavioral interview questions that you construct, the importance does not rest with textbook answers. The importance is found in an applicant's comfort in discussing these situations and whether or not they appear uncomfortable with the subjects presented. A great organizational health fit will answer these scenarios with ease, while someone who is engagement challenged will struggle to find the words and concisely express their approach.

While we are talking about interviews, we may as well take a poke at some organization's sacred cows: the group interview.

Quite bluntly, group interviews, even the two-on-one variety do not work. They become an exercise in presentation skills and not a good approach to finding good organizational fit candidates. If you are looking for someone who will be good presenting to groups, great. However, if you are looking for a more balanced score card of skills and competencies, kill the group interview process. Replace it with multiple interviews held by different people who will all be asking the same questions.

Successful Organizations Never Compromise

Another important facet of successful organizations and those extremely concerned with organizational health is that they never compromise their standards to get a position filled. When organizational health is foremost as a business strategy, you will never hear "he was not perfect, but we need to get that job filled".

No compromise means that you will not take a warm body or a pulse no matter what other pressures you face. A bad hiring decision or a knowing compromise today will create organizational health issues for you for years to come. Refer back to your problem team members. How many of them would you hire again, or how many would you like to re-interview and test those engagement and organizational health competencies?

On an operational level, you will need to take a stand. You will need to tell your human resources department that you need more candidates. You will need to rerun your job advertisement. You will need to tell your boss that you haven't found the right fit yet. All difficult, but all extremely necessary to guard your existing organizational health and ensure team member engagement is not harmed.

Trimming the Non-Engaged

The final look at talent management being used as a driver for organizational health deals with how to handle the disengaged.

One of our customers, a high-ranking executive, was tasked with turning around a pretty dysfunctional environment. Productivity was poor, morale was in the tank, customer service was a lost cause, and they were a mess. He was also told to fix a series of engagement issues plaguing his department for several years. Those issues were identified clearly on a couple of years of engagement survey results.

So, he did what he was directed to do and attacked some of the engagement issues. He turned that environment around in short order. But there were a few casualties. Not the fatal kind but the loss of job kind. Several very toxic supervisors were reassigned, marginalized, and ultimately left the organization. The remaining team members let out a huge sigh of relief and some openly applauded the addition through subtraction that occurred.

Ordinarily, this would be the end. That executive would be heralded for the turnaround and for the progress towards fixing engagement issues, but this is not a fable. This is real life in complex organizations.

The complex part of this story resides after the toxic team members were removed. They took the opportunity of their departure to share some very stinging and unfair comments in their respective exit interviews. A couple even went to the CEO via email with their complaints of unfair treatment. This organization then adopted a case of very selective memory. Forgotten was the guidance to clean up the department. Forgotten was the command to do whatever it takes to fix engagement, morale, and performance.

Now that department manager had to endure an "investigation" conducted by the human resources department into his style and practices. They found nothing, but just the lack of support was chilling.

So why share this? The story above is not designed to scare anyone or prevent doing the right thing related to poor team members, but rather to fully disclose the reality related to getting rid of team members. Sometimes there are consequences. Sometimes there are obstacles, and sometimes there are even slanders to your character and motives.

The grossly disengaged and toxic team members must be removed from the working environment. There is no skirting this issue and no other approach will work. You can try to move them, spend a great deal of resources in training them or trying to reach them, but all those strategies have very little impact.

The bottom line is this: If they are toxic and disengaged, they don't want to be there. They will never want to be there. They will never contribute in a meaningful manner. They must go.

Chapter 3

*N*eeds Fulfillment

"One of the oldest human needs is having someone to wonder where you are when you don't come home at night."
Margaret Mead

In 1943, Abraham Maslow broke new ground in describing the pyramid of human needs. His five-tier approach may well be the most cited and used work related to needs, reactions, motivation, and satisfaction. Later, and after additional research, he added three move levels to his model.

For our purposes, we are going to apply the Maslow Hierarchy of Needs in a modern context and use it to drive a large part of healthy organization strategy.

A Little Background on Maslow

The original five tiers are presented visually in a pyramid. This purposeful approach highlighted the need to build need fulfillment from bottom level to top. Ultimate motivation, and therefore performance, would be achieved when all levels of need were satisfied. The converse view is that performance and motivation is limited because needs were unmet or unsatisfied.

The bottom or base level of the pyramid is described as physiological needs. This lowest level of need includes breathing (duh!), food, water, shelter, sleep, and a few more bodily needs. I have a couple of friends that would include beer, jet skis, and credit cards to this list. Quite simply, the bottom of the pyramid is the minimum amount of commodity and function needed to live.

The next level up on Maslow's model is safety. This is the most straightforward of the levels and the easiest to understand. The descriptors for this level include security, law and order, stability, and being free from fear. As easy as this one is to understand, it is also the level that has changed the most in meaning and application. More about that in just a bit.

The third and middle pyramid block is social needs that include a sense of belonging, love, affection, relationships, acceptance and connectivity. Just as the safety level has changed a great deal, this level has changed very little in meaning and application to a healthy working environment.

One of the most misunderstood levels of the pyramid appears next. Just the word *ego* tends to send a lot of people spinning in various directions. Images of arrogance and aloofness often are created, but this could not be further from the truth. Ego needs, the next level of need and motivation, relates to how we are validated and includes recognition, reputation, achievement, and status. Ego needs tend to be very powerful motivators.

The final and top level of the Maslow Hierarchy of Needs is self-actualization. When describing this need in leadership development programs, I have seen more head-scratching, eye-glazing looks than with any other discussion point. Maslow did us no favors when he used the title "self-actualization." This final tier of need and motivation relates to how you see yourself and where you are at. The description words he used include development, personal growth, challenge, and new experience. As it is the highest point on the pyramid, it will be the most elusive of the motivational factors and needs.

As noted previously, Maslow added three more levels after his initial findings. Those levels are cognitive needs, aesthetic needs, and transcendence (sounds like this will make your head explode). The cognitive category includes our intellectual and knowledge acquisition needs while aesthetic is concerned with our need for beauty and pleasing surroundings. Transcendence is not as mind blowing as it sounds. It is the need to guide another person through self-actualization. This is often seen in the role of parent or mentor in a working situation.

So, what the heck does all this classic psychology and needs mean to a healthy working environment? That is the simplest of all responses. Many organizations fail to meet the needs of their team members and therefore impact, in an adverse manner, the engagement and motivation of their organization. Meet more needs and your organization will be healthier. Stymie the meeting of needs and you will have an unhealthy working environment.

Chapter 4

𝒩eeds Fulfillment-Compensation and Benefits

"Do your job and demand your compensation; but in that order."
Cary Grant

No one expects you to provide food, housing, sleep, clothing, and other necessities for your team members. To meet physiological or baseline needs, we need to convert our understanding of this need level to one of the compensations needed to pay for those things. For our purposes, physiological needs relate to compensation, and we then trust our team members to use that compensation to provide those base needs.

The answer here is easy; just pay everyone in your organization more. Right?

No. That could not be further from the truth. This is not about how much you pay but the perceived equity in the amount you pay them.

Pay Equity is Not Up to You

The equity in compensation is not up to your definition. That should be a shocker to you if you have invested significant company resources to demonstrate how you are paying people compared to other organizations, or if you who have spent a tremendous amount of time analyzing jobs and tasks to ensure those people are being compensated fairly.

Pay equity is a perception. A perception that is defined and owned by individual team members. You can influence that perception, but you can never change it directly.

Consider this example: A long term team member has been promoted several times and given the minimum level raise each time. She has been an outstanding team member and you get great value from her.

Your company then hires a hotshot from the outside at the same organizational level at about $20,000.00 more per year. Despite your naïve belief that no one will know about this, it will become public knowledge soon enough.

Your long-term team member will now have a perception of inequity based on the new hire made at market conditions. Her performance, engagement, and value to the organization will be adversely affected if not corrected or addressed.

At this point of this narrative, some of you will be tempted to say something like "that's the way it is" or "it happens all the time" or even "she should have negotiated her promotion better." And in each of those statements, you are right, but you have to consider the larger and greater picture of organizational health and long-term performance.

Pay and compensation also has a relativism factor.

My ex-wife and I used to reminisce about the days when our household income was about $30,000.00. We were just married, had no bills, and always had some money in our pockets to go out and enjoy the world. Fast forward to two kids, a home, two cars, student loans, and credit cards and even earning five times the household income is not cutting it. Compensation is relative to life stage and personal choices made by the team member.

Also consider a single team member with a straightforward lifestyle being paid $40,000.00. Their perception of compensation equity will be favorable. At the same compensation level, a mother of three with a mortgage and car payment will have an unfavorable perception of compensation.

Both examples are designed to illustrate the relativism of compensation. On the surface, it appears to be a phenomenon that you cannot possibly influence, and it is entirely driven by team member choices. Some of that is true, but you do have some ability to moderate compensation relativism.

Winning the Compensation Game

As mentioned earlier, this is not about giving everyone an across-the-board-raise. This is about how your compensation is communicated and how you can get rid of some of the elements described above.

First, do know how your compensation stacks up locally, regionally, and nationally? You don't have to be at the top end of the scale, but you do have to be in the scale. From there, you need to share that information with your team members. Frequently tell them where their compensation ranks with competitors. Show them the studies and research. Be proud of where you are at in the scale.

Secondly, provide team members with some sort of reporting or statements about the total value you provide them. List not only the base compensation but the benefit contributions and the value of all other organization provided perks. This statement has great value in taking the focus off of base level pay and providing team members with a more accurate reflection of their monetary value.

The third approach to managing this need set is providing your team members with access to financial counseling or financial management programs. Consider that most companies provide some type of employee assistance program with a psychological counseling component. Why not offer some financial management resources to help team members overcome the stress associated with their money management? This will help you offset some of the relativism and comparisons that afflict many team members.

One final strategy for dealing with compensation need fulfillment is to connect compensation with individual contribution. Look at what each position or type of position contributes and share that information with team members. This provides team members with a sense of equity based on what they contribute to the organization.

Collectivism Breeds Mediocrity

The World of Work organization, in a 2010 study focused on the impact of compensation and other monetary rewards found:

> When the impact of different categories of rewards programs on engagement was studied, it was discovered that base pay and benefits had the overall weakest relationship with the organization's ability to foster high levels of employee engagement and motivation compared to incentives, intangible rewards and quality of leadership on engagement.

A long-time senior leader in the hospitality industry once told me that the worst decision his organization ever made was to pool the tips of valet attendants. He told me in no uncertain terms that the pooling created a mediocrity among some of the team members. Star team members drove the entire shift's tips while some team members purposely passed on opportunities to provide great service to their guests.

Many organizations, some of them very successful, offer some form of bonus or profit-sharing incentives to team members or management. Very frequently, this is done through a broad application of a flat percentage of profit or the even distribution of a fixed amount among pool participants.

While noble in intent, these types of approaches do not achieve the desired results and can actually serve to disengage and embitter star performers. Imagine for a minute that you and your department contribute significant revenue and profit to an organization while another department is a drain on earnings. How will you feel when that department manager receives the same incentive as you get? How will you feel when you split tips with the waiter that provides an eighth of the service you provide?

A program designed to encourage contribution and engagement will have the reverse effect. High performers will be discouraged, and mediocrity will become prevalent.

The answer here is quite simple. Make sure compensation extras like incentive pay, tips, and bonuses are connected to individual contribution and not spread equally through a total population. Yes, you want to encourage teamwork, but this is not the tool used to enhance collaboration and oneness. If you are given a bonus pool to split, make sure it is divided based on successful contribution and not blindly distributed. If you collect tips, give them to the individual that earned them.

In the same manner also, make sure any base pay raises are done based on contribution levels and not just across the board. When everyone receives the same three percent annual increase, your contributors and star performers will become disengaged and disenchanted with the process.

Benefits that Provide Benefit

Have you ever test driven your own benefit plan? Did you like the experience? Was it easy to use?

In a world full of copays, deductibles, lifetime caps, out of network providers, and covered events, it is no wonder our team members are confused as to the advantage of our benefits. This does not even consider the potential additional complexity added by the Affordable Care Act. Nothing has the potential of draining morale quicker than benefits that are overly complex and impossible (at least from the perspective of the team member) to use.

Strategy numero uno is to make sure your benefits are easy to use, easy to access, and easy to understand. Kill the techno-speak that only human resource people seem to understand and speak in clear terms about what a benefit provides. Don't make your people go through a lot of hoops and multiple portals while providing the same information multiple times, just to get a benefit that you have committed to provide.

The other strategy associated with benefits is to make sure they are meaningful and valued by team members. How do you get that information?

You ask them.

Ask them what they want. Give them some options. Ask them what would really add value. Do they want educational benefits? Do they want a health club? Do they want more life insurance? Do they want childcare? Stop assuming and start asking prior to putting together your next benefit package.

Chapter 5

$\mathcal{N}$eeds Fulfillment-Safety and Economic Security

"There is no security on this earth; only opportunity."
General Douglas
MacArthur

Continuing on the needs fulfillment path, we will look at Maslow's second level on his hierarchy: safety and security.

Maslow was born in 1908 in Brooklyn, New York to Jewish immigrant parents. With this as historical backdrop, his view of safety and security was framed from the post-industrial revolution period and with emerging activism surrounding mine safety, factory health issues, and child labor. It was certainly not uncommon in the first fifth of the twentieth century to send a canary down a mine shaft to determine the levels of toxic gas.

Fast forward now to a post-great recession world. Safety and security is and has become, mostly about economic safety and security. Therefore, satisfying that need in our team members will take a multi-faceted approach in order to assure them that their jobs are safe and we, as an organization will be there tomorrow.

This phenomenon also explains why many team members flock to public sector jobs when they become available. Layoffs and shutdowns in the public sector are far rarer than in the private sector where downsizing, rightsizing, and staffing level studies have become the norm. Ever seen the line around the block when firefighter tests are announced? Do you know how many applications are received by police departments? This is no accident as people search for higher levels of economic security and safety.

Share Your Financial Data

Don't ever assume your people don't care about results and financial strength. Don't ever assume your team won't understand financial results.

They do care, and they will understand. When you make a bazillion dollars in net income, they take notice. When you lose a bazillion dollars, they equally take notice.

The lesson here is pretty easy. Share your financial results with your team members in the most transparent, straightforward, and honest way possible.

In a recent article and study published in the Harvard Business Review, Bill Fotsch and John Case wrote:

It's surprisingly easy to generate this kind of engagement among employees when you make the economics of the business come alive by sharing some key financial numbers. It's an open-book approach: people begin to watch these indicators. Then they figure out how to move them in the right direction.

A while ago, for instance, a global travel-management company picked three representative U.S. branches to pilot open-book methods of building engagement and improving performance. The company's team identified a critical financial number—site revenue minus direct site costs, known as direct profitability. Branch employees then began meeting every week to review these financial results, brainstorm ideas for improvement, and forecast future results.

In the past, the company's front-line travel counselors had behaved pretty much like employees everywhere. They did a competent job, but they didn't worry about the financial implications of a changed itinerary or a new hotel pricing policy. Now—engaged in the business of improving their branch's numbers—they began spotting opportunities an owner might think of. A customer-relations rep in St. Louis, for instance, contacted vendors to recover money lost due to hotel no-shows and canceled flights. Over the first few months she collected $189,093—a significant savings for the company.

Each pilot branch generated several such ideas, which they then shared with the other two. At the end of the pilot period, the experimental branches had exceeded their profit budgets by 10%, 17%, and 20%, resulting in more than $1.7 million in incremental earnings. None of the other U.S. branches hit budget that year.

The objective, as identified by Case and Fotsch, is to convert employees to owners. Not in a literal sense, but rather, to instill in those team members a greater sense of ownership and contribution based on the open sharing of financial data.

This is the old analogy of ownership comparing the farmer to the hired hand.

For our purposes, the increased ownership will be a bonus (and a significant bonus it is). We are going to focus on the increased safety and security developed when our team members see our organization doing well, or at the least, overcoming our challenges and recovering from any downturn.

The best practice here is to share a summary of financial data related to company strength and use language that is common to team members and not typical CPA-eze. Share this regularly and use a small bit of narrative to highlight significant strengths in the organizations financial structure.

Another practice is to segment financial data for their area of influence. This is not new, but typically this information has been closely guarded and held by managers who were directly accountable for their department or branch. Start sharing that information and talking about what it means. Give your team that sense of security when you are contributing to the success of the organization.

Share Your Story and Celebrate History

Many of your organizations have a rich and interesting history. Even in new startups, the history of the thought, planning, ideas, and entrepreneurial spirit is an interesting read.

History creates a bond of stability and stability equates to the need of security from our team members. Create, share, and celebrate your organization's history. Tell its story. Talk about the founders. Be open about the struggles and how they were overcome.

The richest form of this story sharing will involve multi-media and high production values. Be proud of who you are and where you came from; share that with your team members. This should not only be a part of regular discussions with team members, but it should also be included in any new team member orientation or onboarding activities.

In addition to the enhanced sense of security and safety, the sharing of your history will also grow team member's pride and attachment levels. This is true in companies and families alike. Celebrated history is a strong attachment tool.

Discrimination, Harassment, and Hostile Work Environments; Oh My!

Another element related to the safety and security of our team members is the working environment itself.

Do team members have a reasonable expectation to be free from discrimination and harassment? Should they come to work and not expect hostility or bullying from a team member or supervisor?

Well, of course they should, and we have known that since the mid-1980's. After all, we show them the video annually and sign the form. So, all is okay, right?

Not really.

Showing the video, doing the annual training, and signing the policy forms are a nice first step, but there is more to it than that.

For a team member to feel increased safety and security related to an absence of harassment and discrimination, they must take their commitment seriously and consistently. We will cover this in a bit more depth in the section devoted to ethical congruence, but as it relates to safety and security needs, any organization must walk the walk and not just go through the motions.

All complaints of harassment, bullying, and discrimination must be taken seriously and when investigations are complete, the sanctions must be severe and consistent. Nothing will rock someone's sense of security and safety when it becomes public knowledge that a known harasser is welcomed back into the workplace.

Simply don't tolerate any of those behaviors. This is a time for you to focus on the "what happened" and ignore the "who did it." Deal with these issues seriously, swiftly, and harshly. Don't let someone who is bullying, harassing, or discriminating drag down the engagement and morale of your team.

Old School Security

A final look at the need for safety and security will be more of a throwback.

Unfortunately, incidents of workplace violence and domestic violence spilling into the workplace are on the rise. They are also becoming more lethal. In fact, the US Bureau of Labor Statistics reports that there are over 700 fatalities per year related directly to workplace violence.

No company or organization can ever prevent all of these or even mitigate a situation where someone is determined to do harm to another person. So, what we will choose to look at is the sense of physical security and safety

We have all seen instances where the wrong people get into a building or where door locks have been defeated, but visible physical security has the impact of enhancing the belief of safety. It is a lot like the illusion created by living in a gated community. Any elementary grade school student worth his or her salt can scale the gate or squeeze between them with ease, but yet the residents feel safer because of the gates.

What is the real value of coded door access, company badges, security entrances, and the like? It creates a sense of security and safety for both team members and customers alike. The real security and safety value may be nominal at best and inconvenient at worst, but the sense of security is the real value.

Equally valuable as physical security elements are items such as background checks and drug testing. It will not keep criminals and drug addicts from working at your place, but it certainly enhances the appearance of a secure and safe working environment.

Chapter 6

*N*eeds Fulfillment-Social Interactions

*"My wife told me if there is any rumors about me,
it better be about politics
and not about my social
life."*
Lou Holtz

Funny what I remember about my past jobs in the corporate world.

I don't remember the major achievement of key metrics, promotions, conflicts, major consolidations, centralizing of functions, system conversions, or big presentations in the board room.

I do remember the company picnics, happy hour gatherings (give me a break; it was the 80's, that's what we did), holiday parties, softball leagues, and impromptu fun events in which we partook. One of the most memorable was when my team presented a skit at a company-wide meeting. We planned it for weeks and talked about it for weeks after. Another great memory was a department only gathering that ended with a rousing game of touch football. Great times and great memories.

This is also true about all the church, social, and community organizations in which I have participated. The impromptu or unscripted social interactions have the greatest lasting memories.

The objective of this little trip down memory lane is to point out the incredible importance of social interaction related to healthy working environments and moving beyond typical engagement strategies. As the third highest level of human connection, Maslow identified social needs and the need for connection as having great significance. After securing the basics of food, water, shelter, and safety, humans need to

interact and build social circles.

Humans are built for social interaction and connection

with other humans and not to carry out their existence in an

isolated and solitary existence. In 2009, Dr. Riitta Hari and Dr.

Miiamaaria V. Kujala published an important study linking social

interactions to overall physical health and brain health that

included:

> Human beings are social by nature and live in
> continuous interaction with each other and the external
> world. Within this framework, the omnipresent action–
> perception loops lead to the creation of an inner world,
> the embodied mind, which strongly relies on the
> interaction with the environment. The mind, with its
> many levels, is socially shaped and reconstructed
> dynamically by moment-to-moment interactions.
> Furthermore, a large part of human cognition is off-
> loaded or outsourced to the environment.

Some Baseline Facts on Social Interactions

While all of you will agree about the need to have social

interactions as a part of a healthy life, some of you will

disconnect when we begin talking about this in the context of a

working environment.

There is a large population of you reading this now that absolutely thinks there is no place in the working in environment for socializing. Time is money and yakking is a waste of time. This is work, not the weekend. That's okay. You are hardwired in your personality like this, and in some respects, it has probably served you well. Hopefully, you will see some differences in approach in the coming sections.

Another important baseline to consider is that the healthiest relationships and social interactions some people have may be those at the workplace. Think about a person who has utter chaos in their life. Their home life and after-work life are just a train wreck of dysfunction. While at work, the people are mostly normal, happy, and well- adjusted. Do you think that person craves the healthy interactions and social environment at work? Of course, they do, and they need it.

Traditional Engagement Strategies on Social Interactions

The common approach to meeting social needs within the framework of engagement strategies was to produce top-down interactions. These would take the form of either a team member rally or monthly birthday lunches or daily meetings to start the day. These are all well and good and serve some purpose, but they are largely missing the mark in meeting the social needs of your people.

The reason that these models fail is because they are driven from the top. This means they are led or directed or designed by the leadership teams and not by the team members themselves. There is then an assumption that the corporate message of gratitude, great results, or just plain rah-rah will somehow create a social connectivity with team members and enhance their engagement levels.

What team members really want and what they are provided related to social interactions are rarely the same. While engagement strategists look for ways to put more team members in a room at the same time, team members actually are looking for more relaxed and intimate social settings in which to interact. It is really hard for team members to socialize and connect at a five-hundred-person rally with high quality production values but much easier to bond during a bowling league match or at a lunchtime book club meeting. This really becomes the difference between talking *at* and talking *with* someone.

Quite simply, rallies, birthday lunches, and big team meetings don't enhance the social needs of team members.

Don't Shush Your People

We had the opportunity to work with an organization that did not allow one group of team members to openly interact with another group of team members. This was not done out of some security concern or because it would cause a disruption in the flow of service to customers. It was done because the leaders in the two intersecting departments didn't want their team members visiting and socializing. It caused resentments and most team members were absolutely confused about why this rule existed.

The rule no longer exists.

As discussed previously, people are wired to be social and to interact. The two primary methods of social interaction are via physical touch and communication. Since physical touch is a workplace taboo (and rightfully so. We don't want a bunch of hugging going on here), communication becomes the remaining tool for personal and social connectivity.

A pretty good-sized group of your team members will want to talk to each other. And if it is not distracting to others or taking away from the overall quality of the work, this interaction should be encouraged. Never shush your team members or discourage their interaction as it could absolutely destroy their primary motivation in coming to work, social connection.

Rather than shushing (love this word. Reminds me of kindergarten), effective team leaders will encourage interaction, engage in it themselves, and say things like "it seems pretty quiet in here today" to stimulate some social interaction.

Another consideration is when you allow your team members to eat lunch and go on breaks. If you spread these out too far and only allow one or two to go at the same time, you may be dampening the social needs of your team. Look liberally at how many you can have go at once and allow the team to have input on when they want to have breaks and lunch in order to keep their social circles intact.

Create Opportunities for Ad Hoc Social Interaction

The first rule here is to listen to your team members.

Don't assume that you have the answer and that a company picnic will solve all social needs and engagement woes. Really listen to what your team members want.

Some of the most common replies will be to have open meetings without supervisors, managers, or executives to discuss issues and interact freely. As long as this does not turn into a classic gripe session with no boundaries, this is a pretty healthy approach. You will want to limit the time for these types of interactions and appoint someone to facilitate each meeting to keep it moving and make sure people are not talking over each other.

Another relatively common request is to create small affinity groups based on shared interest. These groups include the bowling league team, softball league, book club, or charity support group. Whatever it is does not really matter as long as it is driven by the team, and everyone has equal access to participate in an affinity group. The affinity group will provide the smaller scale social interactions that macro-sized company sponsored events never will.

When was the last time you decided to close early or take an extended lunch and invite everyone on your immediate team out to celebrate something? Not some regularly calendared event but a spontaneous trip to the local pizza place for lunch. Just you and them. No agenda. No company slideshow. Just socializing and having some fun. Pick some milestone or metric or maybe just use the surviving the end of a month. This becomes a priceless social needs meeting for many of your team members.

Leveraging Social Media Connections

The final strategy for meeting social needs involves emerging technology and a decrease in traditional social interactions. It also is designed to appeal to the highly network conscious and millennial generations of your team.

As a companion to, and not a substitute for, traditional social interactions and connections, wired social media offers an opportunity to jump start relationships and dialogs with team members that do not have ordinary or regular avenues to interact.

For those of you who have Facebook and Twitter phobia, relax a little bit. You are not going to over-disclose your deep personal interactions and idiosyncrasies but rather just create some avenues for increased humanization and interaction.

First, some basic ground rules and then, some best practices. Is it okay to let team members know you have a dog, are married, and drive a truck? Sure, it is. Those are the same type of elements you would disclose and share during a conversation or during any other social interaction. Hobbies? Sure.

Is it okay to disclose you are working fiercely to elect a candidate to the US Senate, operate a brothel on the side, and enjoy your fair share of recreational marijuana? Share pictures of your taxidermy collection? No. Absolutely not. Just as with what you would disclose in conversation, there are some things that you certainly don't want to disclose in conversation as well.

The absolute best practice for using social media to connect people and meet social needs of team members is to use an in-house platform. Unfortunately, this often will limit the application of this practice to exceptionally large organizations or those who have dedicated resources available in their ilogy functions to manage and implement such a solution.

:periences when creating internal social networks have

iothing short of spectacular. The creators of these

ny sites use what works best on Facebook, LinkedIn,

, and Instagram and cut out some of the higher risk

associated with public and open social networking. It

team members to add faces to names, meet team

ers in other divisions and locations, and engage in

ssions across normal departmental and geographic

idaries. They get to connect and socialize with team

nbers in which they would not normally interact.

Additionally, these internal social networks can be

onitored and edited to ensure that inappropriate content is not

iresented, and they may be moderated to make sure

comments remain on track and never venture into hostile or

conflict territory. Many human resource and learning

management software programs, as well as common web

content managers, now include these types of social media

plug-ins.

This is all well and good if you have the time and resources to construct such an internal site, but what about the rest of us? Companies and organizations have had good success using some of the features available in Facebook and LinkedIn to support similar types of interaction. These will never be perfect and not everyone has Facebook and LinkedIn accounts, but creating private groups, those in which you control who joins, offer a great starting point for this type of connectivity. It allows for networked contact within a safe environment and discussions for only group members. Another upside of this type of solution is that it is free and only requires someone to step-up, create, and moderate these groups.

Chapter 7

$\mathcal{N}$eeds Fulfillment-Recognition and Appreciation

"There are two things people want more than sex and money; recognition and praise."
Mary Kay Ash

Ego, as described in classical psychology, may be one of the most misunderstood principles and concepts related to self and self-management. Maslow did not add much to clarify ego when he described ego needs as the second highest need and motivational factor.

A lot of the confusion about ego is not really about ego but much more about people who are egotistical or project a way more than healthy level of egotism. We then, almost naturally, associate ego with arrogance and aloofness; two characteristics that are universally disliked in people and hated in leadership.

For our purposes, ego will simply be the construct of something that makes us feel good about ourselves. So, if you do something, anything really, and it makes you feel proud or accomplished or satisfied, it will be ego fulfilling. Go for a long walk and feel good about yourself. That is ego fulfilling. Produce an outstanding looking report with graphics that is widely proclaimed. That, too, is ego fulfilling.

The role of work in ego fulfillment is twofold and operates within the direct proportion of the amount of time people spend at work. Quite simply, because people spend so much time in working mode, they must derive a significant amount of their ego fulfillment needs from the work environment. We cannot be naïve and believe people will obtain their ego fulfillment only outside of work.

Conversely, successful organizations also make sure their team members maintain proper balance between work and other life elements to allow team members to obtain ego meaning outside of work.

Our strategies will focus on a couple of key areas: recognition, appreciation and praise, and meaningful work.

The Double-Edged Sword of Recognition

Everyone likes recognition, right?

Nope.

And in fact, some people are so opposed to public displays of recognition, it becomes demoralizing and dreaded.

This is one example of where traditional team member engagement strategies let us down. Most, if not all, traditional engagement strategies utilize some form of increased recognition of individuals or teams for their contribution. In and of itself, this is fine, but there are a couple of important points to consider.

First, make sure that you are recognizing something that is truly remarkable and strategically important. You should never recognize someone for being on time to work for ninety consecutive days because it is not extraordinary by any measure and it really has no larger, strategic value. This is an area in which you must challenge yourself and your thinking. Does service time (five years of employment, ten-year anniversary) have real strategic value and are they really something to recognize? They have become such an ingrained part of many corporate cultures, no one is asking about what value they produce in the individual or the organization.

If you fail to use this litmus test, you run the risk of providing recognition that will not be valued by the individual and thus not fulfill ego needs. A greater risk involves the skepticism and jadedness that comes along with hollow recognitions that are not thoroughly vetted and connected to true value.

Another miss related to recognition involves permission. Prior to publicly recognizing any team member, we need to ask their permission and respect their answer. Based on distributions of personality types, there are between 25% and 30% of people in any working group that would be identified as introverts. Those people do not like the spotlight or public adoration coming from being called to the stage to receive their plaque. They would much rather hear something privately and go on about their business. An organization can really discourage any kind of meaningful contribution from introverts when they expect to be embarrassed in a public display. Embarrassed would be their descriptor and not yours.

The secret here is to ask them if it is all right to recognize them and, whatever their response is, respect that choice. You might be able to encourage them a bit but if they acquiesce, let it alone.

One of the best models of meaningful recognition is an impromptu and ad hoc version in which senior leadership team members spontaneously and regularly recognize important performance elements and behaviors. To pull this off, simply arm some members of your senior team with some pins, coupons, or cards and tell them to look for positive examples of important behaviors. A great example of this when the company president sees a piece of great customer treatment, he or she congratulates the team member and gives them a "service star" pin and coupon for lunch.

The side effects of this type of approach are very positive as well. This model creates crossover between recognition and feedback (more about that in the next section) and it forces a higher level of visibility from senior leadership team members while connecting them in a more meaningful way to the line level team members. The only caution of this method is not to turn this process into, well, a process. It should not become a competition among senior executives, and there should be no pressure to distribute some arbitrary number of recognitions in a set period of time. You have to work hard to keep it meaningful and valuable.

A final note on recognition. Be sure to make a celebration that really focuses on the individual. Unfortunately, we have seen far too many robotic presentations of the "employee of the month" type of certificates where it sounds like a chore or sounds like we are just rotating who wins the certificate this month. Make it a party and better yet, make it specific to who you are celebrating. If they like horses, use a horsey theme. If they like soccer, use a soccer motif.

The Power of Appreciation and Praise

B. F. Skinner was the pioneer and coined the piece of science "operant conditioning." Skinner was referring to the phenomenon of when someone has an expectation of something good happening, they will replicate a behavior; when someone has an expectation of something bad happening, they will cease the behavior.

We need to think about this in a couple of different contexts. First, the expectation of getting a paycheck is a good thing, but it only provides performance and behavior at the minimum level needed to come back to work tomorrow. The paycheck buys the lowest acceptable level of performance and behavior. Nothing more.

So how do effective leaders and high-performance organizations get their team members to perform at a higher level? They create an expectation of good related to appreciation and positive feedback. That process of unleashing discretionary effort, the amount of performance above minimum standard that a team member can summon, is an extremely powerful tool in successful organizations.

Now it gets simple. How do we create the expectation of appreciation and praise? You provide it and provide it now. The expectation will be created by the consistent application that you apply now.

The ego tie-in is even more simple. When you are praised and appreciated for your work, you feel good. Good about yourself. Ego needs are met.

This process is significantly more powerful than recognition because it is a personal transaction between a leader and a team member. Team members want to please their leaders and the ego fulfillment of knowing they did so is a very strong motivational tool.

Positive Feedback Must Be Delivered Correctly

In my immediately previous book, *__LeadWell-The Ten Competencies of Effective Leadership,__* I spent a lot of ink and forest product to deliver positive feedback in the correct manner and to the correct populations. For our purposes here, a summary of those techniques will suffice.

Positive feedback, those statements of appreciation and praise, must be delivered as immediately as possible after the favorable event. This clearly connects the events and the recognition that the event was valued and positively received. This point also serves to distinguish between recognition and appreciation and praise. Recognition is usually deferred while praise and appreciation are delivered in a timely manner.

Appreciation and praise should be delivered with a tone and approach in which the team member feels the appreciation and praise and does not just hear the words. Be upbeat and truly appreciative when delivering this message. Nothing will kill the power of appreciation and praise quicker than saying it in a grim and flattened manner.

To maintain sincerity, always make sure appreciation and praise are directed specifically to the person and reference the performance or behavior. Not just a "thanks" or "good job" but rather a "thanks for your work with that customer" or "good job on that pricing report."

Make sure you deliver appreciation and praise to all populations in a fair, consistent, and equal manner. What this means is, if a person you don't like does something well, they receive appreciation. When the person that has been a problem performer does something well, they receive praise. Fairly and consistently. All actions that are valued and meeting the standard for performance need to be praised and appreciated.

Finally, you should never connect appreciation and praise with the dreaded "but" statement. "You did a nice job on that report, but the font was a little small" will not work and has no value in creating an expectation of a positive event when positive performance exists.

Work Needs Meaning

The final strategy in meeting the ego needs of our team members is to either make their work more meaningful or to communicate the meaning and value of their jobs more effectively.

The point of meaningfulness is the self-creation of ego fulfillment when a team member has the belief that their work and efforts have real value and contribute to a bigger product. When the carburetor installer understands the impact of their work and contribution to the overall automobile performance, pride and ego fulfillment follow. No one wants their work to go down a giant black hole with no understanding of how that work contributes to a more holistic view of success.

We need to make an important assumption here. Everyone's work has meaning and value. Otherwise they would not be getting paid to do it. Otherwise we would call it play. Paid employment has value inherently just by the very nature of being paid and having market driven terms.

So where is the issue? Although a team member's work has value, many do not know or understand that value. It is incumbent on us to communicate this value and share it often with our team members. Whether their contribution was huge or modest, it was a contribution to the whole and needs to be articulated. The hotel guests loved their stay. Do we communicate that to the housekeeper, groundskeeper, front desk person, and security officer or do we just keep them in the dark about their contribution to this successful customer interaction?

Chapter 8

$\boldsymbol{N}$eeds Fulfillment-Growth,

Development and Meaning

*"Most men lead lives of
quiet desperation and go to
the grave with the song still
in them."*
Henry David Thoreau

Self-Actualization was the descriptor given for the top
level of Maslow's Hierarchy of Needs. He went on to explain
that this was about someone realizing their dreams and
executing their personal potential. Many psychologists have
added descriptions related to potential and meaningfulness.

For our purposes, we will look at self-actualization as
being in your dream job or being on track to obtain your dream
job. A further definition of a dream job means one in that

scope, contribution, title, and organization fit your desires and meet your needs.

With that definition set in mind, is it possible that a greeter at Walmart is a dream job? Sure, it is. As long as that individual it meets the criteria of scope, contribution, title, and organization. As hard as is it for some people to reconcile, not everyone wants to be the CEO. Not everyone wants a promotion. Not everyone wants to be the boss. But everyone desires self-actualization.

Career Matters

Career management and planning used to be a common element in team member reviews and regular conversations. Through the convergence of new paradigms in talent management and an unforgiving economic climate, those conversations became much rarer.

In her 2010 report, Dr. Lori Long disclosed these details from a study of the Deloitte career management program:

55% report program has positive impact on desire to work for Deloitte
62% report they recommend Deloitte to others because of this program
85% report improvement in career development conversations

Those are staggering numbers when an organization invests in career management.

Effective leaders should know what the career desires and expectations are for his or her team members. That is the first step in career management and planning. A leader cannot assume a team member's career goals just by past actions, or worse yet, through preconceived perceptions established by the leader. Often, what we assume about someone's career aspirations could not be more wrong.

So, the real deep mysterious management process here is to (insert gasp) ask your team members what they want in their career. That's right. Ask them. You can use a variety of words but ask them what they want. Do they want promotional opportunities? Do they want to work in another area of the organization? Do they want to do something entirely different? Do they love the job in which they are currently working?

In every leadership program we facilitate, I ask participants about the five common tiers of team member relationships. Those tiers are family status, location of origin, interests outside of work, birthday and work anniversary date, and career objectives. Without regard for levels, most leaders will know most of the family information, most of the where they are from data, some of the interests outside of work and even some of the key dates. Rarely are many leaders in tune with the career objectives and aspirations of their team members, and leaders are missing a huge opportunity to engage them on a much higher and deeper level.

The simple and missing element is the conversation that starts with, "Where do you want to be in the next few years, five years, or ten years?" "What is your dream job?" or "Where do you see yourself ending up?" These discussions are not

occurring.

Career Planning and Mapping

So now you know what they want to be. What next?

To begin meeting the high-level need of self-

actualization, you must partner with your team member in their

career development. Knowing where they want to be is just the

first part and the work on this need is just beginning.

The first thing that you must consider is not thinking in

terms of the traditional linear ladder approach to career

management. That approach was that a team member only

moved up the organization in a very straight-line type manner.

To get from position C to position P, the team member moves

methodically to D, E, F and so forth. You move from team

member to team lead, to supervisor to manager to director to

vice president to CEO.

That pathway approach is arcane and does not meet the needs of the modern working environment. Fewer people desire the step-by-step model and even less desire the rise to the top when comparing quality of life issues. The method that does work is a multiple path and multiple target approach in which several career options are outlined and mapped. This strategy will serve people far better without pigeonholing them to a single career objective point.

Next, you will have to put on your analytics hat and do a little gap analysis. You know where your team member is and what his or her skill sets look like. You know where they want to be and where they want their career to take them. Now you need to plot out the gap and find the steps needed to get there. This can include some education, skill enhancement, achievement of job standards, improved image, enhanced relational connectivity, or even some diversified job functions.

These gap steps now provide your team member with some very personal objectives to meet. No longer is the team member only working for the betterment of the company but now is also working on individual growth as well. This transition will achieve a huge increase in morale, motivation, and engagement for that individual team member. As you partner in their career growth, you will gain a partner in your operational objectives. You give them a little more in this area, and they will give you more as well.

Beyond this career planning and mapping, you want to add career management and the steps to get there as part of your regular interactions with that team member. Ask them what you can do to assist them and ask how they are doing with some of the steps the two of you outlined to get there. Facilitate as much as you can and encourage the rest.

As a best practice, career management and planning should be done as an independent process separate from all other talent management functions. When it is added as part of the performance review process, it will often lose importance and get lost in an operational discussion. Make this valuable process completely a stand-alone.

Diversification and Rotation

Major league baseball's Hall of Fame pitcher Greg Maddux loved to talk about hitting. His hitting. He wasn't particularly good at it, but he loved to talk about it. In his 23-year career, he hit .171 with 84 runs batted in and 5 home runs. Not stellar stuff, but it is what he wanted to talk about. A legacy point for Mr. Maddux is his Nike commercial titled "Chicks Dig the Long Ball."

The point of this little side trip through baseball history? He liked to talk about the most diverse and rate part of his game. Maddux did not talk about what he got paid to do extremely well, but he raved about the part he longed to do more of and the part he wanted to become better at.

A different job can be as good as a better job. A different job is often a better job.

When career paths and career matrices are not appropriate or not available, that doesn't mean self-actualization needs should be ignored. In some environments, the best possible solution is to look at making work more meaningful, and thus satisfying the self-actualization need, through either a diversification or rotation strategy.

First, let's look at job diversification. Not many things can be more discouraging, demoralizing, and just a drag more than doing the exact same thing with the exact same people in the exact same place over and over again. Most stress and morale studies will cite repetitive work as the most common and most significant contributor to burnout, stress related illnesses, and overall poor production. Fortunately, this is a dynamic in which we have significant control.

I had the opportunity to visit Fry's Electronics recently. Actually, I went there twice, and a single feature struck me and stayed with me. A pleasant young man helped me with choosing some microphones and what would work best for my needs. I went to look at a competitor and returned 45 minutes later. Upon my return, the same young man was in the greeter station at the front of the store. I queried him about this in a joking manner, and he indicated the rotation helped them avoid burnout and keep them fresh.

You can do the same thing. In fact, most successful organizations do this type of regular job diversification. Someone will work the phones for a few hours, move to the front counter for a few more, and then work on answering email for a few more. Wash, rinse, and repeat. The objective here is clear, and the results are even clearer. The freshness of job diversification provides a higher level of team member satisfaction and provides meaningful meeting of needs related to self-actualization. The sheer exposure to different functions, people, and surroundings will keep negativity from creeping into team member's minds as well.

The challenge here will rest with the leader. There is obvious comfort in knowing the same people are doing the same thing. You have put your talent where it belongs and matched jobs to people, so why mess with that? It will also force to the leader to invest in cross-training and be more creative with scheduling and resource management. Nevertheless, the rewards are high, especially when career planning may be sketchy or unavailable. The bottom line here is to look at job functions and work diligently on providing regular diversification of tasks and surroundings.

The second tenet of this section is one that, unfortunately, is rarely used. It will be seen occasionally within the framework of a leadership development program, but the applicability of programmed job rotations goes well beyond creating generalist leaders.

Job rotation is the systemic movement of team members to new jobs as their permanent assignment. It differs from job diversification because rotation is a temporary change while rotation becomes the norm for a fixed period of time. A team member works in customer service for six months, and then moves to provider relations for six months, followed by a move to finance for six months. The amount of time above is arbitrary for example purposes, but best practices indicate a timeframe of somewhere between six months and two years. You are looking for the sweet spot between developing expertise and effectiveness in a function while avoiding the point of potential burnout or dissatisfaction. Over time, this process will also allow the leadership team to build a much more nimble and efficient response to resource needs because you have created an army of generalists that can work in any company function.

Again, looking at best practices, the natural starting point for this is to begin with the senior and middle leadership teams and cascade the process down to supervisors and line-level team members.

Meeting self-actualization needs comes on two levels. One is that you are preventing the dissatisfaction and demoralization associated with long-term repetitive functions that will completely destroy the self-actualization of team members. The second front of this approach is providing team members with opportunities to clarify their self-actualization needs and to see other avenues of career satisfaction beyond their existing department.

A job rotation strategy, when fully implemented and functional, will also reduce silo behaviors often present between departments of large organizations and improve relational strength across the full company spectrum.

Learning Creates Actualization

Another powerful tool and strategy for meeting team member's self-actualization needs is to provide learning opportunities for them.

Slowly, tuition reimbursement programs are returning from the abyss of the Great Recession. Prior to that global economic event, many organizations offered their team members the opportunity to attend college level programs and would pay for or reimburse them for the costs. The overall merit of these programs has been debated for decades and there is no clear answer to traditional views of return on investment related to tuition reimbursement.

What is clear is that providing an opportunity for a team member to learn and grow has a significant impact on their self-actualization. Learning new and different things promote their ego value and achieve the self-actualization that job tasks and functions cannot provide.

Dr. Winslow Burleson in the Journal of Human-Computer Studies writes:

> Developing learning experiences that facilitate self-actualization and creativity is among the most important goals of our society in preparation for the future. To facilitate deep understanding of a new concept, to facilitate learning, learners must have the opportunity to develop multiple and flexible perspectives. The process of becoming an expert involves failure, as well as the ability to understand failure and the motivation to move onward. Meta-cognitive awareness and personal strategies can play a role in developing an individual's ability to persevere through failure, and combat other diluting influences. Awareness and reflective

technologies can be instrumental in developing a meta-cognitive ability to make conscious and unconscious decisions about engagement that will ultimately enhance learning, expertise, creativity, and self-actualization.

To the point of Dr. Burleson, does your internal training rise to the litmus test of facilitating self-actualization or does it only focus on short term changes in skill or behavior? Take a close look at your internal offerings for learning and development and see if they rise to this bar. Most do not, and team members have to seek external sources for self-actualization-based learning. Thus, the need for tuition reimbursement or educational assistance programs arises.

The most compelling evidence of the value of a tuition reimbursement program comes from Colleen N. Flaherty in her 2007 research report where CSP represents the company in the study group:

> For those hired after September 1, 1999, participation in CSP is significantly higher for workers in a non-supervisory role and is increasing in wage (Table 11). Participation in CSP has a large effect on retention: it reduces the probability of separating within five years by 50 percentage points.

Other studies show similar results. Providing for small negative financial impact while creating an environment to achieve self-actualization will have positive returns related to turnover, morale, engagement, and productivity.

One point of best practice associated with tuition reimbursement programs, their administration, and the impact on team member's self-actualization needs is that the more complex and difficult to maneuver you make a program, the less likely it will be to fully meet self-actualization needs. Very simply, if you build a tuition reimbursement program full of applications, approvals, front-end payments and grids of eligible classes, you will be missing the capture of self-actualization with a large population of your team members.

Consider this example for a moment: a lower level team member desires to continue her education and get her degree. She is highly motivated, engaged, and a high-performing team member. Your tuition program reimburses the team member after successful completion of a class. The team member does

not have enough disposable income to front the college costs.
The risk here is self-evident. She could easily lose her
motivation and even develop a sense of defeatism and at a
minimum, look at your tuition program jadedly. Her hope for
self-actualization and your desire to have self-actualized team
members has been lost.

Look at your program. Is it user friendly? Does it appeal
equally to all levels of team members? Can everyone access
it? Does it offer mutual benefit to the team member and
organization?

The simplified best practice statement for tuition
programs includes simple approval, agreement by the team
member to reimburse costs when not completed, and a general
grid of classes that offer mutual benefit. Remember, the harder
you make it, the less likely team members will utilize it.

In the absence of a tuition reimbursement program, your
organization can create learning tiers for team members. This
would provide progressive achievement of learning levels and

be more favorable in creating self-actualization in team members. For example, you have a required customer service training program for all team members. You will want to add an intermediate and advanced level for team members to work at as well. This allows team members that are closer to self-actualization to achieve their goals and objectives. It also allows team members to customize their learning needs to their career goals.

Organizational needs training does extraordinarily little to satisfy self-actualization needs and in some cases reduces morale. If you have ever heard something like "I can't believe we have to go to this ridiculous (fill in name of program here) training" or "We just did something like that last year" or even "We are doing this whole training because (fill in name of team member here) sucks at conflict", you are not touching self-actualization needs. For corporate training to meet their highest motivational need, it needs to either match training the team member desires or training in which the team member sees value outside of immediate performance or compliance.

Here, the solution is quite simple. We need to do a better job of marketing internally offered training related to team member value, and we need to offer the types of training that our team members request. That doesn't mean that if your team requests a yoga class that you have to go buy mats and hire a yogi but it does mean you have to reach out to them and see what they want to learn. Once you begin this path, you will start to tap into their self-actualization.

Mentoring as an Actualization Tool

A one-on-one relationship with a key senior leader or respected peer meets team member needs on a variety of levels. The connection to self-actualization in mentoring is through providing an individual environment to share career aspirations, learning and growth needs, and to provide coaching that is often unavailable or focused only on performance within the bounds of a department or division assignment.

I will not attempt to address everything there is to know about mentoring in this section but rather offer a few best practices in creating an environment where mentoring assists meeting self-actualization needs for team members.

First, mentoring is an individual connection between team member and mentor that is designed to transfer knowledge, wisdom, and experience from the mentor to the team member. The ultimate objective of mentoring is to create team members that are more prepared for succession and more aware of higher level and bigger picture challenges and develop cross-boundary relationships within an organization. If a team member desires those outcomes, mentoring becomes valuable in tapping into self-actualization. If a team member does not want those things, it will have the same outcome as the mandatory corporate training discussed in the above section.

Step one is to always know and inquire about the team member objectives. They must match or closely match the desired outcomes of mentoring. If not, mentoring will not be valuable to the team member or organization. If there is a good fit, mentoring will help unlock the self-actualization motivation.

Secondly, please understand mentoring is not for everyone. You must focus your efforts and resources only on those team members that are not only desirous of the outcomes but also have satisfied their other need sets. It makes no sense to mentor someone and try to appeal to their self-actualization if they are struggling satisfying their ego or social needs. For a team member to be effectively mentored, all of the baser needs must be met or in the process of being met. Think about putting a $400.00 designer suit on a pig. It really doesn't look much better and it certainly irritates the pig.

An often-overlooked part of successful mentoring is formality and adding systemic elements. Far too many mentoring processes fail because we treat them with an "I'll get with you when we have time" or an approach of open flow interaction. Successful mentoring is programed with participants meeting with mentors at least monthly and using a structured outline of discussions. This is not to say there shouldn't be flexibility to discuss current issues, tackle challenging team members, or tell stories, but there must be a structure to ensure the participants and the organization are achieving the desired outcomes and producing values.

The best models of mentoring use mentors at least one level up from team members and mentors that are not in the same functional area. The reason for this is that it directs mentoring discussion beyond current performance needs and really into the development of the team member. It also provides value in giving team members a wider world view related to an organization.

When higher level mentors are not available, using a successful peer in another operational area is also an option. As an example, if a divisional manager cannot mentor the supervisor, a supervisor with a great reputation for development in the finance department could be used. The same expectations should be in play even if a peer is used instead of a more senior leader.

The final note on mentoring is kind of a bummer. Not all mentors and team members fit well together. Build a system to check in with team members being mentored and see how it is working. Don't be afraid to change mentors if they have not established a good relationship or if objectives are not being met.

Charity Starts at Work

A final strategy related to achieving self-actualization and moving beyond standard engagement is unconventional.

First, a reality. Not a new one. One we discussed in earlier sections. Not all team members want a promotion. Or a million dollars. Or your job. Or the corner office.

In fact, many team members desire to make a difference. A difference in their community and world. They want to make the lives of others better and leave a legacy not related to job title but a legacy of help and compassion. This is also a growing trend as more and more team members, especially those in younger generations, seek satisfaction from what they donate and what volunteer hours they log.

This population of team members will see self-actualization in what they can do for others and how they can help others. Think of Sister Teresa or Mahatma Gandhi. The highest motivational factor for these people is how they can help and where they fit in making the world a better place.

The good news is we can assist them and achieve self-actualized team members in the process. Many organizations have discovered higher levels of engagement, satisfaction, and retention through adoption of volunteer programs and team member driven charity efforts.

A JA Worldwide (Junior Achievement) report from 2009 cites several studies and summarizes them marvelously:

> Company-sponsored volunteer programs have many benefits to the sponsoring company. One of the most

measurable impacts EVPs have is on the attitudes, productivity and job satisfaction of company employees. According to the study Good Companies, Better Employees (Tuffrey, 2003), some of the outcomes of effective EVPs include:

An improved rating among employees for their employer as a place to work compared to other companies (63 percent saying above average or one of the best, compared to 57 percent before the program was in place).

Increased job satisfaction levels (64 percent fairly or very satisfied among all employees, compared to 62 percent before; satisfaction among volunteer program participants rose to 67 percent).

Increased positive word of mouth among employees about their employer (54 percent saying they would speak highly of their employer, compared to 49 percent before the program was put in place; among volunteer program participants, the rate rose to 57 percent).

Higher retention rates for employees who participated in volunteer activities than for those employees who did not. Additionally, employees who participated in volunteer programs appeared to be more prone to pursue promotion and development activities in the months following the participation in the volunteer programs.

In terms of attracting new employees, approximately 62 percent of workers 18- to 26-years old would prefer to work for a company that provides opportunities for them to apply their skills to benefit nonprofit organizations. Professional growth is part of the reason why these so-called "GenYers" want volunteer programs. About 76 percent of young workers said that volunteering helps them hone their leadership skills, and 75 percent said volunteering lets them develop skills they can use at work (Deloitte, 2007).

These numbers are eye-popping. Increased volunteerism equates to higher satisfaction, lower turnover, and enhanced reputation. Winner.

Our role in this element is facilitation. Not to always lead but to facilitate the opportunities for volunteers and charity work. Not to just pick our favorite causes but to really see what is meaningful to the team.

We will discuss input and voice in detail in the next chapter, but for our purpose here, the bottom line is you need to listen to your team members. Listen to what is important to them and how they would like to contribute and volunteer. Don't just automatically assume that cleaning the park that is important to you is important or has any value to them.

A couple of examples to consider. I remember with crystal clarity, an effort by a company in which I was an executive to help build homes. Great cause, but my team didn't

want anything to do with it. They had their own ideas and

thoughts on charitable campaigns and none of them signed up

to build low income housing. After seeking their input, I made

the risky decision to support their idea. We achieved nearly full

participation and all they talked about for weeks was their

efforts related to their chosen charity. We bucked the

organization but achieved a great deal of engagement and

satisfaction that we could not achieve by trying to support the

dictated cause.

Many churches spend a lot of time talking about why

their level of volunteerism is so low and why their congregants

do not support their chosen missions. This is repeated

frequently across church size, sect, and location differences.

Not horribly long ago, a church asked for support in building a

new wing. Without any comment on the need, I was not

connected to this new construction project in the slightest. I

wanted to help the homeless. No one really asked me what I

wanted to do, and I ended up not supporting the construction project. And so, it goes. Time after time in an endless cycle repeated in most churches across the continent. Pick a project. Try to gain support. Complain about the lack of participation.

In both personal examples, the missing ingredient was asking what the team, or in the case of a church, the congregation, what they wanted to support. If your organization is using a top dictated or committee chosen charity or volunteer opportunity without seeking input, you are missing out on potential support and thus not meeting the self-actualization needs of team members.

A couple of successful strategies to consider are using some type of direct team member input through a couple of elimination rounds to see what they want to support. Start out with open comments, narrow it down to a top ten, and then provide two or three options based on the plurality of support. This will make sure that you are reaching the maximum number of people to support the causes that resonate with them and not just getting cursory support for a company sponsored initiative.

Another great strategy to meet self-actualization needs through volunteerism and charity work is to incentivize volunteer hours. That can be done as simple as providing recognition based on volunteer hours during a month, quarter, or year, or as sophisticated as granting paid time off when performing volunteer work. The approach there balances the amount paid with the value achieved via public relations and corporate image and the enhancement in team member satisfaction.

There is no one-size-fits-all approach to using volunteer, community, and charity work to grow job satisfaction and engagement, but we do know that the traditional model of company dictated causes does not work particularly well.

Chapter 9

*Ɔ*nput and Voice

"We need a variety of input and influence and voices. You cannot get all the answers to life and business from one person or from one source."
Jim Rohn

If I have heard it once, I have heard it and read it a thousand times.

"Management doesn't listen to us". "Management doesn't care about our ideas".

The dreaded evil management and their failure to listen. It is very frequently cited on traditional team satisfaction and engagement surveys as the (envision a Family Feud host here) number one response related to complaints or reasons for disengagement.

After studying this phenomenon extensively, my take is a bit different. I believe management does listen to team members but does a very poor job of validating that listening. Further, organizations often create false mechanisms for soliciting input that do a very poor job of engaging all team members.

It isn't that management doesn't listen; it's that management doesn't listen in a particularly effective manner and the communication after listening is poor at best.

Input Equals Buy In

Input, ideas, feedback, and commentary from team members have several distinct values. First, it allows leaders to see unintended consequences of their decisions and actions. Unintended consequences are those results which are usually a negative impact and not known or anticipated by the leader at the time of the decision. Team member input provides valuable insight into the "what ifs" that leaders do not see and often even provide voice to customers as they are closer to transactions than leaders.

Besides its ingredients for a beverage, Coke has another recipe for success. From their webpage:

> To encourage a work environment of open communication and to effectively solicit and leverage innovative ideas, we engage in frequent dialogue with our associates around the world. Such dialogue provides us with valuable information, increases awareness, promotes business strategies, shares successes and opportunities, and solicits employee opinions. For example, global associates and bottling partners have contributed ideas to major initiatives, such as our 2008 Beijing Summer Olympic Games activation. And, employee input was a key ingredient to our Company's Mission, Vision & Values.

Another value of input is the perception of voice. Voice is defined as the merit and value of individual team member input. We seek input, and the team member believes they have voice in the organization or in the direction of an issue or challenge.

The real value of input is the buy in.

Management consultants have been throwing the phrase "buy in" around for decades. It has been used to describe a combination of higher ownership, accountability, and effort provided towards execution. The problem is and has been that the key ingredient for buy in has been largely ignored.

First, let's define buy in. Buy in is a cumulative set of attitudes and behaviors that result in a team member having a higher degree of ownership, accountability, and effort towards an effort or cause. It can also be described and defined as a team member's degree of agreement with, support of, and belief in the righteousness of an organizational direction or decision. The complexity of buy in exists in combining beliefs and attitudes and then actions. In a simpler form, when a team member buys in, they will exert greater effort and have more pride in the accomplishment of a task or set of tasks. Buy in is indeed a desired outcome.

Rather than concentrating on the actual composition of buy in, organizations and their leaders have been trying to incent, cajole and sell buy in. Thinking somehow that a slick slide show at a team meeting will somehow garner support, enthusiasm and buy in is naïve at best and ignorant at worst.

When a team member participates in any organizational process such as decision making, problem solving, strategic planning, and interviewing, their buy in is dramatically increased. In a very straightforward manner, participation and input equal buy in. Stop trying to sell your ideas and spend that time in seeking input and you will see team member buy in rise dramatically.

To further validate this important concept, think about a couple of examples. The first is the comparison of two organizations currently engaged in strategic planning. One organization uses a top down version in which managers, directors, and executives plot the course of action for the coming year and establish key goals for their department and the company. They then roll out the strategic plan and goals to the team members through a kickoff meeting (complete with PowerPoint slides). In a second example, another organization engages their team members prior to any formal strategic planning. They ask team members what the organization should fix and concentrate on and seek input on where improvements and changes can be made. From that input, leaders assemble the information into objectives and action plans. Which one of those two organizations will have higher ownership and support for that strategic plan? Where will buy in be highest? Those are easy questions. The organization that seeks input will have much higher strategic plan buy in.

Here is a final example on a much smaller scale. Ten out of forty portfolios are underperforming, and the management team is concerned. The manager and a key supervisor have crafted a plan to move some resources and team members around to attack the need and are planning to announce this decision via both a team meeting and a series of emails. Without any input from team members, what will be the degree of support for this initiative? Will the team be supportive or is there a chance for push-back and wading into a sea of unintended consequences? There will be more on how to get input in the upcoming sections.

Validating What We Hear

As mentioned earlier, I believe management and individual leaders do a pretty good job of listening to team members. We can do better but we do listen.

Where we often stumble is how we validate, or more accurately, don't validate what we hear. We hear, but our team members don't have any reason to know that we heard them.

You hold a team meeting and attempt to solicit input and ideas about an issue. You hear from some of your team members with some feedback. You take some notes. And after that. Nothing.

As identified before, many organizations solicit input and feedback from team members using engagement and satisfaction surveys. Your team members provide numeric ratings and comments. And after that. Maybe a meeting reviewing key report highlights but more likely, nothing.

Your company has a policy to provide a small bonus to anyone submitting an idea that is implemented and saves a couple of bucks. A team member submits an idea. Not a particularly good idea but an idea, nonetheless. That team member receives an automatic email response thanking her for her submission to ideas@bigcompany.com and after that, nothing.

A team member is struggling with her immediate supervisor and decides to talk to that supervisor's manager. That manager listens and promises and beyond that interaction, nothing.

As the above examples point out, it is no wonder that our team members don't think we listen to them. We listen, but we provide no signals to communicate that we are really hearing what they are saying.

In interpersonal communication, listening must be validated to be completed. Think of this in a circular diagram where there is data being transmitted and data being received. The completion of the circle is the validation of the received data. There must be a signal provided to indicate we have heard and received the data. It can be a head nod, rephrasing statement, or even an "uh huh".

With interpersonal team member input and suggestions, we must utilize a less subtle approach to validation. First, we must always thank them for the feedback or suggestion. This, in and of itself, is a powerful validation and reinforces that you appreciate and value their comments. Without this part, a team member will be left wondering if you truly heard them.

Secondly, we must provide an action statement and commitment. This must be closed-ended by stating a firm date or time in which we will respond back or complete an action. Without the closed-ended commitment statement, a team member will think you are just pushing off their comments. There is a huge validation difference between "I will get back to you." and "I will get back to you by Friday at noon."

Then finally, we must follow through. If you commit to trying something, examining an idea, or investigating a process, you must do so. Or in the absence of being able to do it, explain to the team member why it did not happen.

Putting this all together, a perfect validation statement to interpersonal team member sounds like "Thank you so much for the idea, and I will look at it and get back to you by Monday of next week." Another approach would be "That is great input and thanks for sharing it. I will get someone to look at it and have some information for you when we meet again (assuming this is a fixed date and time)."

In regard to validation of input, AT&T used this approach successfully:

> The companies that regularly earn high employee engagement tap that knowledge by asking employees how the company can earn more of their customers' business and build the ranks of customer promoters. And they don't just ask; they also listen hard to the answers, take action, and let their employees know about it.

> For example, AT&T has built a digital infrastructure enabling all employee suggestions to be logged online.

A small, dedicated team regularly reads and triages the suggestions, sending each promising one to a designated leader or expert who is obligated to consider it and respond. Employees can see the progress of each suggestion and log comments. Other companies have developed systems that enable employees to "vote up" or "vote down" the ideas suggested by others, with the best ones getting the attention of the leadership team.

With other input sources, we must use different validation methods. If we receive an email suggestion or other types of input, we must respond to it with the same criteria used in interpersonal validation (i.e. thank, commit to action, and follow-up). The important point here is that a response comes from a real person and not an automatic responder and the validation email must be prioritized. When an email comes to you that you must forward on to someone else for review or implementation, don't just blindly forward the correspondence. Send a separate note telling the team member where the suggestion or input is going and stay connected to ensure follow-up and action. One of the best practices we ever saw in action required 24-hour response timeframes from anyone receiving a suggestion or input from another department or manager. This process ensured the team member always knew who was looking at his or her input and kept the team member from believing the communication fell into a giant black hole somewhere in the organization. Please also remember that your team member will be consistently looking to you for the validation, and it really doesn't matter to them to whom you chose to forward the email.

Validation of input received in a public forum is a little trickier and may require you to multitask a little. If you get some feedback or an idea in a meeting, be sure to thank the team member and make a note of who said it and the context of the information. After the meeting, make a point of individually validating the input as you would if you heard it in an interpersonal setting. This also allows you the ability to clarify the information received and seek any other feedback about the idea.

Use special care to never dismiss or invalidate a comment heard in a meeting or public setting. It takes enough courage from team members to speak up, and the last thing you want to do is to snuff out their spirit. Once they are humiliated or ignored in a meeting, team members will not be heard from again.

While we are about taboo topics, let's spend a moment talking about poor validation methods that reinforce the belief that we do not listen to our team members. The first method to avoid is the "we have already tried that" mantra that sadly, is all too common from the mouths of some managers. The message that you are sending is that no matter what the feedback, you have tried it or been there and done that. Very dismissive.

The other validation technique to avoid is "we will never get that approved" or any form of attributing non-action on positions above you. Your team members know better and they very quickly see through your lack of courage in presenting their idea or sharing their input. Again, very dismissive. A final point of poor validation to consider is the "it's not in the budget" line. Again, don't disrespect your people because they know better. They have seen many times that budget exceptions are made and money was spent that was not designated in the budget.

This brings us to the elephant in the room: reality. What if the feedback or suggestion you have received from a team member is just ridiculous? Absurd. A non-starter. Impossible. Never work. Crazy train stuff.

The easy thing to do is call it as you see it, and label it accurately. Unfortunately, that will ensure you never hear back from that team member again, and the risk you run is that the team member with today's crazy idea will hit a winner next time. So, you can't afford to be overly dismissive or condescending.

What you must do is thank them for the input, tell the team member you will review it in some detail, and get back with them with a closed-ended commitment. When the time or reckoning comes and you must tell the team member you are not using their idea, you will explain in some depth why it will not work in your operating environment. Be patient and thank them again for taking the time to provide you with some input. Remember, it is not about this current idea or feedback, it is about all future feedback you will get from that team member.

Seeking Better Input

Besides doing a more consistent and better job of validating input, leaders should create more conducive environments for obtaining input, feedback, and ideas. To start this discussion, we must make a significant paradigm shift.

Rather than concentrating our efforts on only being better recipients of input and validating team member's comments, we need to begin creating environments and processes to actively solicit their voice.

The easiest method to solicit better input, feedback, and ideas from team members is to conduct regular recurring one-on-one meetings. Successful leaders have used these forums for decades to build rapport, have team member development conversations, and just discuss the happenings of the day. For our purpose here, we will use these meetings to get input that you would not receive in any other meeting format.

If you have ever thought about the lack of input you get when you have a staff meeting or brainstorming session, you need to continue reading. Depending on the work environment, an estimated 40% to 50% of people will not contribute publicly because of their personality and personal preferences. No matter how safe you make the meeting or what kind of relationship they have with you, they are not going to speak out. It is not that they don't have ideas or input; it is because they are wired to listen and process rather than open up publicly. Some have experienced past ridicule, some are self-conscious about their communication style, and even more are just built to not be in the spotlight. Before you get too judgmental here, please remember it is just how they are built. You can't change that and the more you press them, the quieter and more withdrawn they will become.

However, that same population of people who will not comment in a group situation will gladly share input with you individually. In a safe environment. In a one-on-one meeting.

Let's look at a few more logistical elements of individual meetings and how to stimulate quality input. First, before you wig out and scream "I have 140 employees, I can't possibly meet with each one individually," you are only to meet with your direct reports. You may have 140 employees, but you only have eight managers and you will be meeting with them. The best corporate and organizational cultures then cascade that leadership behavior to have the eight managers meet with their three supervisors who then meet with the line level team members. This ensures that every level has equal voice and equal access to individual meetings with their leader.

These meetings are not designed to add a huge time burden either. The best models of one-on-one meetings are to use 30 minutes twice per month. You know your people and environment best; so, you can describe the best frequency and duration, but this is the best practice.

There is a population of leaders out there that have said "I don't need one-on-one meetings because I have an open door and talk to my direct reports almost daily." And they do, but you are talking about issues and current challenges only. There is little to no meaningful discussion of long-term strategic issues, team member development, or seeking input and feedback. That is why these meetings are an absolute necessity.

Scheduling and conducting the meetings are not enough to get good, quality feedback. You also have to say the right things and ask the right questions. Use phrasing such as "How do we deliver better service?" or "How do we fix this issue so it doesn't happen again?" or "How would you schedule the team for best coverage?"

While using that type of language, you want to avoid any individual opening that would taint or drive the input you are getting in a direction. In doing so you want to avoid saying things like "Here is what I was planning on doing; what do you think?" or "My idea is this, but I am interested in your input?" In both of those cases you are going to pollute the team member's input and force them into a situation to either agree (most likely) or disagree with the direction that you have already outlined.

I just finished watching a segment on CNN covering some civil unrest in Missouri. The reporter was interviewing several citizens after some rioting and asked a young man what he thought about a solution. He articulated a need to consolidate the many municipalities surrounding the metro Saint Louis area to give residents a clearer understanding of the rules of engagement and who is running what. Million-dollar input. On point and valuable.

The challenge was that he was wearing a backwards baseball cap and missing a front tooth.

Sometimes the most valuable feedback and input we receive comes in packages in which we would not ordinarily choose to engage. Sometimes that input doesn't speak English very well. Sometimes it is unattractive. Sometimes it comes from people we don't like. The point is that we need to park our prejudices and preconceptions of people and look at all input with blinders on our mind's view. We cannot afford to dismiss any input because of who said it or what they looked like or sounded like.

Getting Something Out of Brainstorming

If you are still committed to using various types of group meetings to obtain some input or meaningful feedback, try a little different approach.

First, before you conduct the meeting, give participants ample time and notice of the overall subject and the individual questions that you will be asking. This will provide team members the opportunity to think and process some information and their perspective prior to the group meeting.

Secondly, you will want to offer an alternative method to provide input prior to the meeting. Allow your team members to contribute via email before the meeting if they are more comfortable in doing so. You could even consider requiring their input on those items prior to the meeting so you have a full slate of input prior to any public vetting of the information.

Finally, when conducting the group meeting, acknowledge all the input you have received and be careful to not allow anyone to openly dismiss or ridicule any input that is heard or shared.

Technology is Your Friend

The final approach to seeking better input and voice from team members is the use of technology. Seeking input in the twenty-first century is easier now that it ever was, and we have a wide variety of tools available to us to seek input from our team.

The easiest method is one in which the leader sends an email asking for input about an issue or challenge to every team member. For this approach to work, the tip is for the leader to follow-up once and maybe twice to make sure every team member has responded or has had an ample opportunity to respond. This method of soliciting input is especially attractive to the more analytical and thoughtful team members who do not prefer to speak out in meetings. As discussed in prior sections, make sure you validate these responses with thank you notes back to the team members to demonstrate you value the input.

Another set of tools available to your fingertips is the use of on-demand surveys and polls. They can be as simple as a one question poll with live time results or a more complicated multi-question instrument. I am not going to do your Google research for you, but rest assured that you have dozens of inexpensive and easy to use options available for just about any need.

A little riskier approach to using technology in the solicitation of input is the use of message boards and discussion groups. These hosted solutions are available in commonly used social networks such as Facebook and LinkedIn and are also becoming more and more prevalent in human resource and learning management software packages. These discussion groups allow someone to pose a question and then receive input through threaded responses. If the issue or request for input is sensitive, you must use some caution on how the group is accessed and viewed. In most discussion groups, you can control who sees what and you need to review those setting carefully. This approach is best when you have a smaller and more mature working group that is conditioned to using this type of technology and is comfortable in accessing social networks.

As an easy and low risk trial, open a LinkedIn group for your team. Mark it as a private group and invite your team members. Pose a benign opening question and see what level of input you receive.

Strategic Input

You have a small army of electricians and you are beginning work on your strategic plan for the upcoming year. Or you are looking at the overall vision and mission of your company and you want some input.

In a well-meaning manner, you ask "What should the key strategic goals for the coming year be?" or "What is your vision for the company?" or even "How should we maximize our position as a market leader?"

Crickets.

Nothing. Zero. Silence.

Over a period of years and several strategic planning cycles, many leaders have abandoned any semblance of seeking input to strategic direction because of a lack of meaningful input from team members.

Here again, it is not the lack of desire to provide input, but rather the questions that we ask that will dictate the quality of that input. When we ask high level questions such as those above, there is no reasonable expectation that team members will contribute because those terms do not resonate with their world. It just doesn't make sense, and they have no reason to digest and disseminate the questions.

To get some key feedback and input on strategic objectives and direction, try translating questions to phrasing and framework that makes sense to team members. Use queries like "What can we do better?", "How can we sell more product?", "What can we do to make this a better workplace?" or "What can we do to deliver better service to our guests?" These types of questions will register at a far more practical level with team members and give you some key information that you can then frame in strategic planning processes.

As a reminder, anytime a team member believes they were contributory to the planning process, the more likely they will embrace it and work harder towards the outlined objectives.

Buy in complete.

ate a high level of

onnection to the workplace

e demonstrating interest in

interest. Not superficial

her a deeper connection

d aspirations.

adership excellence, he

pay attention. They care
touch on a personal level,
nce their success as much
ey know when to push
line: The best leaders
– or inspire them do those
em feel better (and make

dence on the impact of

self-reflection. Have you

lieved was interested in

ake you feel? How did

to please that leader?

t?

Chapter 10

*P*eople Focused Leadership

"If your actions inspire others to dream more, learn more, do more and become more, you are a leader."
John Quincy Adams

A common set of questions on most engagement and satisfaction surveys is about the team member's relationship and views about their immediate supervisor or manager. The answer to these questions is very telling and influences the answers related to compensation, career growth, and input. The bottom line here is if the view of supervisors and managers is poor, the rest of the survey results will be poor. If the view of supervisors and managers is good, the remaining results will tick higher.

This is a clear case for the impact and role of leaders in engagement. Your team members work for you and not the company, and to them, you are the company. You have the daily influence on their morale, motivation, and overall engagement.

In his bestseller, *First, Break All the Rules*, Marcus Buckingham provides clarity to the manager and team memb dynamic:

> The talented employee may join a company because its charismatic leaders, its generous benefits, and its world-class training programs, but how long that employee stays and how productive he is while he is there is determined by his relationship with his immediate supervisor.

One of my favorite shared stories during leadership training involves a friend of mine who is the manager of a la hotel front desk operation. When asked about how he likes job, his response is that he enjoys it immensely but does n like the people.

Those leaders that want to cr personal motivation and emotional c will spend a significant amount of tim their team members. Real, genuine "How are you doing?" interest but rat with team member's lives, needs, an

In Jeff Schmitt's "Forbes" article on le makes the case thusly:

> Most important, these leaders about their people and stay in knowing their inner lives influe as any guidance. That's how t and when to pull back. Bottom make their reports feel valued things that'll ultimately make th your organization run better).

There is one more piece of evi leadership interest that requires a littl ever worked for someone who you be and cared about you? How did that m that affect your motivations and desire Did you want to leave that environme

We pose those questions in all of our leadership development sessions, and uniformly, we hear from people who have worked for that type of leader; their strongest motivation was to not disappoint that leader or let her or him down. They did not want to leave, and in fact, the memory itself creates some strong feelings about that leader and that particular working environment.

Demonstrating interest in team members takes time. Not that team members are that complicated (many are) but rather you need to go at this process in a methodical method and show them that you are trustworthy with your interest in them. Some, based on your history with them, may well be suspect of your motives if you have never cared about their kids, dogs, interests, and lives.

It is easy to use a triage type process approach, show interest, and move into a higher quality relationship with team members. Start with finding out some information about a team member's family composition. Married? Children? Pets?

Ages? Names? This is pretty simple stuff and common in many conversations. "Tell me a little about your family." or "What is your family like?" or "Can you give me a little insight into your family and home life?" are pretty common queries to spark this discussion.

The next level of interest is to find out what your team members are interested in outside of work. I know that some leaders really don't care or worse yet, they want their team members solely focused on work, but the reality is that our team members have diverse interests and passions outside of work. Here is a case when you do some quality listening to pick up clues and use your power of observation to see those things that capture a team member's interest. Look to see what kind of pictures are on a desk, a lapel pin that indicates a group or charity, some branded or logo laden dress, what they are reading during breaks, or even what they talk about with other team members.

Thirdly, we want to find out about the team member's location of origin. Where are they from? What brought them here? Most people have a significant emotional connection to where they were born and where they went to school. Tapping into that information will dramatically increase your ability to have future interactions and provide you with a great deal in which to follow up.

The fourth level of team member interest is a direct connection to a previously covered subject. What are their career aspirations and objectives? What do they want to be and when? Discussed in detail, this level of interest in team members demonstrates a long-term view of the team member relationship and a genuine interest in their longevity and success with the organization.

The final level of demonstrating interest by a leader is probably the easiest. Those leaders that are genuinely concerned with morale, high performance, and engagement know and celebrate the work anniversaries and birthdays of their team members. Don't misinterpret the work celebration.

This is not about having a parade or grand party on someone's

birthday but rather an acknowledgement, recognition, and a

personally signed greeting card. One of the most kept and

displayed memorabilia that team members cherish is that

birthday card from the boss. These gestures provide great

value with truly little investment other than some time and

effort.

As a footnote to the birthday and working anniversary

section, the group birthday parties on the third Friday of each

month and the name in the company newsletter for

anniversaries do not cut it. They are fine but achieve little

related to engagement, morale, and performance. This is a

case where individual action by the leader is most important

and valued; and a leader cannot defer their responsibility to a

social committee or human resources department.

All five of these levels of information have two common

threads and an incredible amount of power associated with

them. The first commonality is they are unique and individually owned by each team member. There is no plurality here. Just the traits, interests, and characteristics of that individual team member. The second thread is the power thread. Each of the five levels of team member interest is very important to that team member. In that, the power.

So now you have all this information (family composition, interest outside of work, location of origin, career aspirations, and key dates). So, now what?

Build Quality Relationships

To tap into the five levels of team member interest, you must demonstrate value in the same areas. That demonstration is produced easily by following-up and asking about the information you have learned.

You found out that a team member's daughter had a softball tournament during the past weekend. You ask about it.

You know a team member is working on restoring a classic car. You ask about it.

You were told that a team member is moving to a new house. You ask about it.

Welcome to Relationships 101.

Relationships are reciprocal by nature. When one side does not reciprocate on the known interests of a team member, the relationship will die. When the follow-up inquiries are provided consistently, the relationship will flourish and grow.

There are also a couple of other considerations to working relationships with team members. After you have built the cursory reciprocal pieces of asking about each other and following up on known information, you must be trustworthy and provide some degrees of forgiveness.

Relationship trust is easy to explain but a shade more difficult to consistently execute. The trust factor in relationships is related to the information you gathered and collected during the demonstrating interest stage of enhancing the morale and engagement of your team. To be trustworthy in this context, you must keep that information to yourself and not share it with anyone and not use the information for unfair advantage. Your objective in demonstrating interest and building relationships is not to obtain data you can use against someone, but rather to gain information you can use to display concern, caring, and emotional connection to the organization. Share information out of turn in a gossipy manner once, and you will not be able to recover the relational trust needed to be an engaging leader.

Forgiveness is a little bit more complex and requires a high degree of judgment. You cannot and must not abdicate your responsibility to hold team members accountable for errors and patterns of poor performance and inappropriate behavior. An effective leader will use corrective coaching when there are failures and mistakes of significance. That will remain constant.

For definition purposes, forgiveness is the commitment to not bring up an issue or hold it against a team member. It is not letting them off the hook for doing it or worse yet, ignoring that it happened. It is not bringing the subject up again and rehashing the event.

There are, however, some opportunities to balance accountability and forgiveness. Openly forgive the small and meaningless things while holding team members accountable for the strategically important issues. This may sound like talking out of both sides of your mouth, but it is not. Can you forgive a typo on a report while holding a team member accountable for the report being late? Absolutely. Use judgment and forgive openly when appropriate.

Early in this section, the word reciprocal was introduced. Two sided. Give and take. The earlier reference was about the flow of relational information but there is another dynamic of reciprocal to consider.

A team member can never view or consider that a relationship with a leader is one-sided or usury in nature. If they feel they are being used with no benefit back to them, you will create jadedness with that team member and actually harm satisfaction and performance. That means, leaders will have to also give in the relationship equation. The leader will have to provide time, empathize, and communicate with team members. They will have to express joy when the team member is happy. Sympathize when a team member is sad. This requires time and commitment to truly build the needed relationships with team members.

Many leaders are painfully effortless in building relationships with others. The five areas of interest, being trustworthy, providing forgiveness, and being a genuine reciprocal relationship partner are sooooooooooo easy. They like people and it shows.

For others, it is harder and even tedious at times. They are not natural at it and in some cases, awkward.

There is great news here. Whether you are a natural or must make it more procedural in nature, the end result is the same. You build quality relationships with team members that bear fruit for years. Don't let a lack of God given genetic relationship building skills hamper you from creating this connection with team members.

Be Engaging

One of the oddest looks I can remember from a senior leader when discussing engagement came when we were talking about his personal leadership style.

He asked how he could improve engagement, and my response was for him to be more engaging.

Seems a bit of a conundrum. Improve engagement by being more engaging but it is true. Grumpy, isolated curmudgeons will not be highly effective in improving the motivations and engagement levels of their team members. Those leaders that stomp through a workplace, saying nothing, with a scowl locked onto their faces will be condemned to poor levels of team member satisfaction regardless of pay and the number of company potluck lunches. Similarly, leaders that are disconnected, hiding in their office, and self-absorbed (work or otherwise) will suffer a similar fate.

So, you must be an engaging leader to improve team engagement.

There are several skills to consider that will improve personal engagement. The first is to be seen and be visible. Get out of your office. Talk to people. Build relationships and demonstrate interest way above those projects in which you are managing. To be seen, in and of itself, has great value in demonstrating your personal engagement.

Secondly, communicate frequently with your team and team members. Not through email, unless that is the only method available but rather through interpersonal communication and the effective use of meetings. Not meetings and discussions for meetings and discussions sake but those interactions that have value and share information demonstrating your engagement level. Your personal communication with team members is also how you reinforce their value and provides you an opportunity to further relational connections and provide positive feedback.

The next skill to embrace being more engaging is simple and often overlooked. Greet your people. Make it a point to say good morning or hello to your team members every day. Consistently executing this strategy will ensure your team members know you value them and value them above whatever is waiting for you in your office. The key with this skill, like many others, is consistency. You must do this every day, when you don't feel like it, and even when you are buried in other work.

I will now channel your mother for the next leadership engagement enhancing skills. Be nice to people. If you need something from someone, say please. If you get something from someone, say thank you. If you make a mistake or say something dumb, say I'm sorry. That is being nice. That is common courtesy. In the hubbub of the modern working environment, it is not so common anymore; but the degree of appreciation when a leader is consistently courteous to team member is high. Team members want to hear those little elements of nicety.

While we are looking at nice, let's also look at what is not nice. Snarky and sarcastic leaders will not generate much enthusiasm related to team member connection. This is also true for those leaders who curse frequently, tell off-color jokes, or mock others. Remember what your mom said. Be nice to people.

The final skill related to becoming a more engaging leader is also simple. Look like you want to be there. A little enthusiasm, smile, and a skip in your step will go a long way to demonstrate you are being engaging. Your smile alone will tell team members that you work in a great organization and you want to be engaged with the company and with them.

Increase engagement through becoming more engaging. Not a conundrum at all. A mantra to embrace.

Cascading People Skills

For complete organizational health and high performance, the leadership skills identified in this section must be cascaded throughout the organization. From top to bottom, these skills must be embraced, used, and become a part of any organization's culture. This cascade will also help to prepare leaders for future succession and eliminate any of the sarcastic "Do what I say not what I do" approach found in some companies.

Far too often, these skills are viewed as something good for a level but not useful in others. The line level managers should be engaging, but the senior executives can ignore the skills or use them sporadically. This approach will ensure that the gains made by leaders are temporary and viewed skeptically.

Each leader, from CEO to part-time supervisor, must consistently model the required behaviors and skills for the highest impact on engagement and performance.

Chapter 11

*E*thical Congruence

> *"It is forbidden to kill;*
> *therefore all murderers*
> *are punished unless they*
> *kill in large numbers and*
> *to the sound of*
> *trumpets."*
> Voltaire

Congratulations on that code of conduct you have. Ditto for the corporate values and a big bravo for the harassment and discrimination policies. Great idea for the ethics training and the 800 number to report lapses.

Those documents, policies, and processes mean absolutely nothing if you do not administer them in a fair, consistent, and equitable manner. Your team members are much more likely to remember the high profile and widely known exceptions you made rather than the original construct and intent of your ethics statements.

Visualize a scenario in which team members believe they operate under a code of conduct and ethics that prohibit harassment. A salesman in a branch office openly berates other team members in his frequent fits of anger. Because he is a friend of the manager and produces a great deal of revenue, nothing happens.

Or another situation in which it is widely known that a vice president curses often, as in every sentence he speaks, and treats company resources as if they were his own. Nothing happens because he is related to the chairman.

In both of those scenarios, will there be an effect on team member morale? A more fundamental question might be to ponder how long the lack of accountability to ethical standards will be held confidentially?

Why Ethical Values Matter

The connectivity between ethical behavior and the engagement and satisfaction levels is clear. The Hay Group and the Ethics Resources Center concluded the following from

their extensive research report:

> Positive perceptions of an organization's ethical culture
> are associated with higher levels of engagement.
> Furthermore, management's commitment to ethics is
> particularly important for employee engagement.

Another view from Gene Shklover in his piece found in

Thinking Integral magazine:

> Employees may first be attracted to a company because
> of the public opinion of the ethics of the company, but
> employee engagement is directly related to the everyday
> ethics of top management and direct supervisor ethics.
> The NBES found that top management ethical culture
> has a 73% correlation with employee engagement; direct
> supervisors' behavior is only 4 points behind
> management at 69%, greatly surpassing employee
> engagement due to the advertised ethical standards of a
> company.

> As ethical conduct positively reinforces employee
> engagement, unethical conduct from top management
> and direct supervisors negatively, rather than negligibly,
> affects engagement. 85% of employees who had not
> witnessed unethical conduct ranked as highly engaged
> compared to 61% rate of high engagement from
> employees who had witnessed unethical management
> conduct. Another way to view the numbers is that
> unethical management results in a 24% loss in
> employee engagement.

Now, my summary of research. Initially, the shiny ethical values are appealing and engaging to team members. As team members see them being skirted, not enforced, and applied inconsistently, team members become jaded and disengaged.

Team members have a significant desire for the rules and values that are applied to them, and which they believe they will be held accountable for, to be applied equally and fairly to all team members in the organization. Neutral engagement is achieved in this equation. Simply meaning, there is no enhanced engagement and satisfaction value to ethical congruence and consistency.

Engagement and satisfaction, and therefore performance and organizational health, begin to slip when team members see cracks in ethical consistency. When one well known exception occurs, dissatisfaction begins to creep in. Several exceptions take place and the level of dissatisfaction and jadedness becomes locked in. Consistent inconsistency in the application of ethical values will lead to a very toxic and disengaged working environment.

There is one other consideration to make on ethical value congruence and that relates to the propensity of team members to embrace personal relativism related to ethics. If they are aware of people "getting away" with an ethical lapse, they are much more likely to test ethical boundaries themselves. See, a thief not getting punished equates to someone more likely to try stealing.

Exceptions are the Enemy

The evil archenemy of ethical congruence is the dreaded exception. Applying a new rule where one is not needed or making something gray when it is black or white.

Most organizations start down a solid ethical path in the administration of their code of conduct or application of their values. They run aground when a senior manager makes an exception based on extenuating circumstances, or worse yet, the identity of an offender. These problems also occur when a line level leader chooses to turn a blind eye based on the same data.

As previously cited above, for ethics to have an impact on morale, engagement, and performance, team members must believe that the same rules apply to everyone and that lady justice is indeed blind to matters of doling out penalties associated with violations. Team members will develop an increasing degree of jadedness, up to and including group toxicity, when they see ethical values being enforced differently for different people.

No one wants to work in an environment where there is hyper-rigidity and no room for creativity and individual thought. That is not the point. Therefore, organizations must decide the policies and code of conduct items which, when violated, they are willing to fire anyone and everyone over. Anyone and everyone is a key concept in this ethical testing.

Do you have an attendance and tardiness policy? Most companies do. They need people to come to work regularly and at the assigned start times. When reviewing an attendance policy through the lens of ethical congruence, you must ask yourself a few key questions. Would you coach, discipline, and terminate a line level cashier for excess tardiness over a period of time? Would you do the same to a vice president? If so, you have achieved ethical congruence related to that policy. If not, you have probably fallen into the trap of exceptions and relativism.

Relativism is the belief that all things are relative. In the example above, tardiness is important for the cashier but not for the vice president. That is actually a pretty easy case to make since one is an hourly team member and the other is exempt from overtime, on salary, and regularly works more than forty hours per week. It's relative.

But not so fast. That is not how your team members will see it. They will see a separate set of rules for different people or distinct classes of team members. Therefore, a review of policies and ethical values must include the litmus test of what will we be willing to terminate everyone and anyone over a violation. This is not about justifying the exception and relativism because that is easy. It is about maintaining congruence for the sake of all the non-exceptions.

Another point of reference on exceptions goes directly to your heart and soul. Effective leaders have those and that is excellent. Empathy, as a leadership skill is extraordinary and valued by team members. When empathy turns into sympathy, it is another matter.

A team member comes to work under the influence of alcohol and is immediately terminated. You have a policy and code of conduct item related to that issue. Done.

Another team member comes to work under the influence of alcohol but spins a great story. One that is of soap opera and reality television quality. Spouse left, abandoned kids, home in foreclosure, and financial issues. If you have been a manager or supervisor for any length of time, you have heard these types of melodramas. So rather than the immediate termination that should follow the behavior of being under the influence, the leader turns to sympathy and grants an exception. Easy to justify based on the extenuating circumstances, but the rippling effects will be felt for decades. You have just taught all your team members to tell a tale of woe, and they will get out of most any bind; exceptions exist for those who are good story tellers.

I don't want to sound jaded here, but some parents have died or had the same critical illnesses three or four times over the course of some team member tenures. Why? Because they knew they could use it to get an exception to some policy or rule.

Achieving Consistency in Ethics

First and foremost, you must be the example of every policy and ethical value you prescribe to others and the ones in which you want to hold others accountable. Model the behavior and values you want to see in others.

What this means is that you, the leader, must be diligent in watching your own behavior and make sure you don't even tiptoe the line in which you would hold someone else accountable.

Another strategy for maintaining congruence in ethics is to avoid granting any exceptions no matter how heart tugging of a story is presented to you. If the ethical guideline is to terminate someone on their tenth absence, then that is what you must do. Not enjoy it, but do it, nonetheless. The most difficult challenge to this consistency comes when the person requiring discipline or worse yet, termination, is a high performing or high producing team member. You are responsible for team performance and now you have to fire one of your best performers. That is a tough spot, but the termination is the correct and needed course of action.

You will also want to audit and review your policies and ethical values to make sure they are absolutely what you want to take a stand on and are willing to lose your best person over a violation. This requires some critical thinking to ensure you are balancing business needs and providing your team members with enough room to make decisions and operate. The best rule here is when in doubt, trust your team member's judgment skills and don't make a rule. The more rules you have, the more opportunities you will have to make exceptions.

At an organizational level, one strategy that has proven effective in creating the appearance of ethical congruence is the use of an anonymous reporting system for ethical lapses or inappropriate team member behaviors. The best of these systems uses a third party to ensure anonymity and confidentiality to the reporting party and tracking to ensure the information is received by appropriate level decision makers.

The jury is still out for the company level strategy in which a chief ethical officer is used. That became a bit of a trend in the early part of this decade but lost steam because of reporting structure issues. The dilemma with this position is not the role, but rather where the role reports. At the end of the day, the ethics officer needs to stay employed, and unless they report independently to the board of directors, he or she will need to satisfy his or her bosses.

The final and most difficult ethical congruence strategy is to take a stand. When you see a lack of consistency in administering the code of conduct, ask about it. Remind people about the consequences of no ethical congruence and the impact it has with team members and overall organizational health.

Risky? Absolutely. But necessary when ethical congruence is not being achieved by any other manner.

Chapter 12

$\mathcal{T}$ransparency and Openness

"A lack of transparency results in distrust and a deep sense of insecurity."
Dalai Lama

Connecting transparency and openness to organizational health and team engagement will look a lot like the previous chapter about ethical congruence and you can make a case that the two areas are very closely related.

For our purposes, we will examine both organizational transparency and the transparency of individual leaders and how both affect team member satisfaction, morale, and performance.

Transparency is best defined as the quality of communication from a sender. In relation to organizations and companies, it is the quality of communications and the belief that all information that can be shared is being shared.

If you believe that all facts are being shared in a timely and forthright manner, it will be transparent. It aids trust and a belief in team members that they can further commit to their organization.

In contrast, if you believe things are being hidden, not disclosed, or purposefully delayed, that is not transparent and has an adverse impact on trust and engagement.

TINYpulse surveyed over 3000 organizations for their global 2013 engagement report. Among their most significant findings was this point about transparency:

> Management transparency is the top factor when determining employee happiness. This finding surprised us too, with management transparency coming in at an extremely high correlation coefficient of .93 with employee happiness. The cost of improving

transparency is almost zero but requires an ongoing dialogue between management and staff. We see an increasing number of companies using transparency as a weapon to attract and retain top talent.

In Warren Bennis' book, Transparency: Creating a Culture of Candor, he says, "studies show that companies that rate high in transparency tend to outperform more opaque ones." He cites a 2005 study finding that a group of 27 U.S. companies noted as "most transparent" beat the S&P 500 by 11.3%. Transparency is not only good for employee happiness but also great for the bottom line.

Every organization should be thinking about how they can be more transparent. It is one of the lowest to no cost initiatives to tackle right away. But of course, it requires an ongoing commitment from management to be more transparent to the very people they so carefully brought onboard. At the end of the day, to give is to get.

The one challenge is the understanding and definition that team members provide to the term transparency. Some will apply it to overall organizational culture while others look no further than their immediate leader. So, we will look at both.

Communicate What You Know

Her office is dark. The door remains closed. You can see through the window that the pictures that adorned her desk are gone. Also gone is the extra jacket hanging on the coat rack.

Everyone knows something happened, but not one official peep is coming from the executives. Just the murmurs and gossipy tones from team members. Was she fired? Did she finally tell them off? Is she alright? What will happen to us? Who is in charge?

For the love of sweet baby Jesus, when someone is no longer with your organization, tell your team members. Not the gory details but tell people that Ms. Smith has left the company and you thank her for her service and tenure. Let them know that her department will be reporting directly to Ms. Jones until a replacement is found and that you will be meeting with the team to answer their questions very soon. Very soon.

Unfamiliar suits are in the office. Driving a rental car. A nice rental car. Not the $19.95 per day version. They were here last week as well. Meeting behind closed doors in the big conference room. Are we for sale? Did someone buy us? Are we being audited? Is the government investigating something?

These are just a few of many examples of how a lack of transparency breeds dissatisfaction and contempt from team members. The team member translation to a lack of open communication is first, that you do not trust them with important information and second, that they are not important enough to have that information shared with them. Those two thoughts can be devastating to team morale and spirit.

An especially important baseline truism to consider is that in the void of factual information, people will make up their own version. This is not an uncommon or unique phenomenon. It happens at home. It happens in interpersonal relationship and it happens in large, complex companies. A team member witnesses some new stimuli (suits in the office, closed door meetings, cleaned off desk) and they immediately reach conclusions based on history and experience. Unless you communicate what is really happening, you are at the mercy of the other voices in the organization.

Here is a simple rule to follow that will greatly enhance transparency: if someone has left, someone new has appeared, you have auditors on your campus, you are talking with possible merger partners, you have hired consultants, or anything that will get your team buzzing, tell them. Tell them in a timely manner and before the event if possible. Don't let the gossipers and fill-in-the-blank crowd dominate the information flow.

Time is not on your side here. You have to get your message out. You don't have the luxury of time to craft the perfect email. You just have to be truthful, to the extent that you can disclose, and forthright.

One other important equation to consider is trust equality. We trust our team members with a great deal. We give them cash drawers, let them interact with our customers, and give them signing authority on checks and documents. Do you think we could trust them with knowing that the attorney general is reviewing some of our emails and we are confident their investigation will validate our position that we did nothing wrong? How about telling them we are looking at possible merger partners and will release more information when it becomes available? Or even, we have hired a consulting team to review our efficiencies and service levels.

The challenge in many organizations, especially the larger ones, is that communication of this type often has to be vetted through the legal or compliance department. Since their job is to mitigate and reduce risk, transparency is often lost. Business is risk and that can never be delegated away to some backroom bureaucrats. Trust your team with a constant flow of honest and transparent information.

A couple of winning practices to consider for improved transparency include the production of management talking points and some protocol guidelines for official notifications and also a note about company-wide publications.

If you empower others to share a message or relay important information, it is important to arm them correctly. Weekly talking points that outline key data that should be disseminated throughout the organization is a great way to ensure that all departments, divisions, and branches are receiving the same communication and are then accountable for delivering these messages. This is your opportunity to make sure everyone knows about the suits in the office, closed door meetings, and the replacement of the popular vice president that recently departed.

As much as I personally abhor policies, the use of a communication protocol will ensure that people understand who is responsible for key relays of data and when they must be performed. If a key team member leaves, who is responsible for notifying all the key stakeholders? When must this be done? Who is in charge in the interim? This is almost a crisis type of protocol without the drama of a natural disaster.

The final strategy for transparency is a thorough review of the purpose and messaging seen in company publications. Often company and department newsletters are produced by a formal communication or marketing function. This is great because it ensures high quality output, but it misses out on the flow of key information, and thus transparency, to team members. If you use a company newsletter, and you should, make sure it is informational and reinforces some of the transparency points identified above.

Be Honest When You Can't Talk

As some of you read the last section, you were hounded by the thoughts of the information you can't disclose.

Is Google considering purchasing your company? Does someone have a sensitive illness or addiction? Are your earnings going through the roof but won't be officially announced until next week? Are you disciplining a team member? Is there an investigation about harassment occurring?

You can't say a word about any of those, and in fact, a couple of them have legal penalties beyond what your organization might impose. Without doing some type of partial truth dance, consider just saying you can't talk about it and will do so when you are allowed.

You can feel free to say what you are authorized to say, but beyond that, even in intimation or innuendo, will serve no good and paint you in a difficult position later.

When faced with a question about a team member's absence, simply say she is on an extended leave and apologize for not being able to say any more.

Leader Transparency

The final piece of transparency is about disclosure level and motives of leaders. This has a large impact on overall engagement, morale, and performance when considering the impact that leaders have on team members.

Relational transparency is the first segment to consider as a leader. As you build more solid relationships with your team members and seek information about them (see prior chapters) you will need to disclose, and disclose graciously and openly, some personal information about yourself. If you ask a team member where they are from and they reciprocate the question, you must provide an open and honest response to their question or the relational interaction falls flat. You must be prepared to share your family status, interests, and location of origin as easily as you expect your team members to share it with you.

We have been witness to many leaders that are exceptionally good at gathering team member information and are even pretty gracious about it, but they become uncomfortable and overly guarded when disclosing their own information. As a gentle reminder, the information you have to disclose is not any different than what you would disclose when interacting with a neighbor or someone at a social event. Get comfortable with it or your transparency as a leader will be in jeopardy.

The boundary of relational transparency is that you will not be sharing any of your challenges, professional or personal, with team members and you will not disclose your career objectives. The reason for that is that the former impacts your credibility in an adverse manner and the later may create a sense that you will not be there for your team in the long term.

The second consideration is an emotional transparency. Please, please, please, before you slam this book shut because you have visualized a tearful disclosure of deep, dark secrets and insecurities, read on for just a moment.

Emotional transparency in leadership is about two safe and benign practices. First, when you have made a mistake or completely whiffed on something, apologize. That's right. Say you are sorry. Indicate you erred. Articulate the mea culpa and move on. This demonstrates a genuineness and human fallacy in you, and it is important to let your team members see it.

Rather than cover a mistake or deny it, own it and apologize for

it.

The second piece of emotional transparency in

leadership is the use of empathy. We have previously

discussed what empathy is and how it differs from sympathy.

When a leader can be connected to the emotional state of a

team member and apply empathy, there is a powerful

transparency into the leader's emotional health and

intelligence. Much more simply, you show empathy to

someone's emotions, it indicates your emotional depth and

provides transparency to you.

One final consideration related to leadership

transparency relates to motives. When someone, peer or team

member, asks for help, are you going to provide assistance for

the value expected or do you have a deeper and perhaps

darker motive in mind? Is this something you are going to use

against someone or maybe share some findings with your

boss? If that is the case, your transparency as a leader will be harmed and the trust equation will be damaged. Perhaps

damaged beyond repair. Never provide support or assistance if

your motive is not in the same spirit as it was requested.

Chapter 13

$\mathcal{S}$ervice Based Culture

> *"In the old world, you devoted 30% of your time to building a great service and 70% of your time to shouting about it. In the new world, that inverts."*
> Jeff Bezos

Although this is near the end of the list of factors contributing to organizational health, performance, and engagement, it is by no means the least. In fact, it may very well have the largest impact on morale and team spirt.

Most, if not all, of the research about team member engagement and its relationship to service culture focus on the impact on service culture of highly motivated and satisfied team members. There is no doubt about the strong correlation between engaged team members and delivering high quality service.

However, we are going to flip the script a bit and look at the impact of a service culture on team member satisfaction and morale.

The bottom line here is as we treat team members well, their satisfaction and desire to be at work improves.

Let's look at a couple of examples that will be capitalized upon later to improve service culture related to team members. First, think about organizations that operate on a 24-hour, seven day a week basis. Hotels, security, data centers, fire departments, and convenience stores. All of them have team members working around the clock and covering all shifts on all days.

What happens when one of those graveyard shift team members has a question about their health insurance? They call the human resources department and get an answering machine. They send an email with no immediate response.

They try to call or text message a manager and get the same treatment. The lights are on, but nobody is home.

Another example is a mortgage company in which the team members routinely work remotely during off hours. They take applications, process loans, and try to correspond with potential borrowers to serve those end customers better. A key application is down, and the team member calls into the IT help desk. What do you suppose they get? Another answering machine. A call routed to an offshore help function.

Meet Team Members Where They Are

Centralization is a great thing. There are economies of scale and companies can build bigger teams of specialists rather than scattered teams of generalists.

The downside is that many centralized support functions such as human resources, purchasing, and information technology are not where the team members are working. The plant is in Tennessee and the headquarters and support functions are in California. Often, those team members in remote locations or in non-banker hours shifts develop a stepchild attitude where they believe they are not truly connected or cared about by the headquarters or day shift.

The first best practice to improve engagement and morale related to service culture is to provide reasonable and genuine access to key support functions physically where team members are located. That means a certain amount of decentralization must occur. Should the assembly plant in Tennessee have its own human resources person, IT person, and purchasing liaison? Absolutely. If there are more than just a handful of people in that location, they should have access to a person and not just a toll-free phone number.

The next best practice and the one highlighted by the examples in the prior section relates to the when service is provided to team members. If team members are working, if the business is open, support functions need to be available to provide service to those team members. Before you shudder at the thought of fully staffing some of your support teams for around-the-clock shifts, consider some issues of scale.

If you have thousands of team members working nights and weekends, it makes great sense to have levels of human resources, information technology, and other support team members onsite and available. The improvement in engagement and satisfaction from those remote operations or non-traditional shifts will be immediate and quickly noticed. They are no longer stepchildren.

Conversely, if your night and weekend teams are relatively small or your remote branches do not have a population to justify in-house support team members, you can utilize an on-call function. This is not a new concept. For years, many organizations have used an on-call manager or manager on duty to cover issues that may arise during off hours. To successfully build greater organizational health and engagement, we are just going to expand that same concept into support functions that provide team members key service.

This model has an IT person, human resource team member, and any other key support function available on an on-call basis. When the team member has a question about a payroll deduction at midnight, a human resources person answers the call. Probably in pajamas, but answers, nonetheless.

The emotional and psychological belief that knowing support team members are available when other team members are working is powerful and very positive. Make sure every team member knows about this level of service and support and it will be received well and go a long way to creating a true service culture.

Courtesy Matters

Most organizations, especially the successful ones, do a really good job in providing courtesy and respect to their end customers. They say thank you, please, and use appropriate titling to that customer standing in front of them. They know that has huge economic and cultural value to be courteous.

With fellow team members, not so much.

I have been married a long time. As of this writing, it will be 30 years. Certainly, no small miracle.

Early on, when we were dating, all of the doors were opened, courtesies were exchanged, and generally, I was a pretty polite guy. Nearly thirty years later, my wife walks to a door and I look at her with the "What's wrong is your arm broken?" glance.

This is not to say I don't care about my wife. I do. Very much so. What happened is a very natural evolution in relationships. I became comfortable in my standing with her and that morphed into a level of complacency where I was no longer concerned with providing the common courtesy that she deserves.

The point of this self-disclosure is to point out that the same process occurs in the working environment. Early in the team member-organization relationship, it is all about being polite and respectful. Best feet forward by both parties.

What happens after that is that team members become comfortable. The organization becomes comfortable with you and your presence and the level of courtesy and respect begin to drop. Even longer into the relationship, complacency develops.

For example, you begin by saying "May I please borrow your stapler?" After a few years of comfort, that request evolves into "stapler?" Add even a few more years, and you just take that stapler from your team member without so much as a grunt.

To a service culture, reinforcing an environment where courtesy among team members is the norm is extremely important. When saying *please*, *thank you*, and *I'm sorry* among team members, it becomes easier to say those words to external customers. It also improves the tone of the working environment, reduces stress, and creates a working culture in which team members want to thrive and stay.

The use of courtesy and respect words should be a standard part of any new hire onboarding or orientation process and reinforced often to avoid the creep of complacency. A far more important way to build this element into your culture is through the example of your leaders. Every leader at every level in the organization, from new team lead to CEO, should model this behavior in every interaction.

Tone Matters

The word tone was used in the above section related to the use of courtesy words and the impact in the workplace. In a modern definition, tone is a quality, feeling, or attitude expressed by the words that someone uses in speaking or writing. It is difficult to define but easy to feel when it is either positive or negative.

One of the characteristics of great service cultures is the concentrated effort in managing tone. Tone in verbal communication, tone in written communication, and the overall tone used with team members and customers alike.

The easiest way to manage tone with team members is to use the same skills that we use with customers when interacting over the phone and via email. This means that we don't use a friendly greeting with customers that identifies the company, ourselves, and asks if we can help them. Then, when an internal call comes through, say "What do you need?" into the phone. That's right. Use the same telephone greeting with team members as you would when an outside line comes through with a customer on the other end.

Is it okay to say good morning on the phone to a team member? Should we identify ourselves over the phone? Should we ask a team member if we may help them? Absolutely. All of those ensure the tone over the phone remains positive and consistent with a service culture.

Another common mistake that many organizations make is failure to manage the tone in internal email. Because email has the lowest richness of all communication channels, there is no avenue to determine tone other than the words on the screen. There is no verbal tone and no non-verbal signals from which to obtain a clue. Just your words.

So, a short, one line response, will be interpreted by the receiver as having a bad tone. Sorry, it's not up to your intentions; it's up to the interpretation of the receiver. You meant no ill will, but they interpreted the tone as being harsh and rude.

The cure for this is quite simple and easy to implement. Just add a tone setting line to begin each email and another to close it.

Urgency Matters

One of the most common team member frustrations relates to the relative urgency of their requests for service and information.

In theory, this becomes one of the easiest service culture and team member satisfaction issues to address. In practicum, it becomes extremely challenging.

Consider the contrast for a moment between having a deadline for 2015 strategic plan elements due to your boss and a request to meet with a team member to discuss some issues in their work life. How do you prioritize these? Do you ignore the team member? Do you tell her that you have a priority item that goes to your boss? Do you juggle both? Lots of questions and very few right answers.

One simple rule to use is to prioritize team member requests with the same urgency and priority ranking as you would with an external customer. If you respond to a customer's email within an hour, you should do the same with your team members. If you always find time for customer meetings, find that same time with your team members.

Team members can see, with crystal clarity, how you prioritize them and their needs. It only takes one or two cancelled one-on-one meetings for them to see your work and the needs of your boss take precedence over them. Treat this equation with reverence and make sure your always demonstrate priority and urgency to your team members.

The Circle of Life

If you hear the theme song to Disney's *Lion King* during this section, it is to be expected.

What can you do with a culture driven by service to team members? Capitalize on it and drive the benefits to the service level to your customers. This is not about how customer service affects team members. It is about how service to team members affect customer relations.

With a service-based culture, you are making it easier for team members to provide outstanding service to external customers. When team members are consistently treated well, they will find it incredibly natural to treat customers well. When that equation is flipped, team members will struggle in reconciling the requirement to treat customers well when they do not believe they are being treated well.

The great part of this model is that when it is consistently managed, it will self-perpetuate. The courtesy, tone, urgency, and overall service provided to team members will enhance the service provided to customers; the service provided to customers will continue to grow because of the service and treatment we provide our team members.

Chapter 14

$\mathcal{F}$reedom

"For to be free is not merely to cast off one's chains, but to live in a way that respects and enhances the freedom of others."
Nelson Mandela

In the rural setting in which I grew up, there was a farmer who owned the fastest horse in the county. In fact, it just may have been the fastest horse in the state.

Problem was he rarely took him out to run. Let him trot periodically on a tether. Brought him to a half-gallop occasionally. But never turned him loose and let him run. He just kept him in the barn.

One day, that horse broke down the stable door and the last time the farmer saw him was running at full stride towards the sunset.

The object lesson here is quite simple. Let the horse out of the barn to run once in a while, or it will leave you.

One fundamental commonality between humans and most of the animal kingdom is the ability to recognize the value of freedom. As the most foundational right, the elation of freedom can be easily observed in any creature that has not previously experienced it.

Don't believe me? Rent Free Willy.

Workplace related observation is what happens when team members are encouraged to operate with maximum judgment and a high degree of freedom. They innovate. They provide great service. They solve problems. They flourish and prosper. And they do it with a great deal of satisfaction and

enjoyment.

The previously cited Hay study writes extensively about

team member freedom but does a genuinely nice job of

defining the scope of workplace freedom. To wit, freedom is

not the absence of boundaries but the ability to create

empowerment within reasonable boundaries:

> If you think you're empowering your employees by
> stepping completely out of their way, you could be
> wrong. The absence of boundaries is not empowering;
> it's limiting. Employees who don't understand how far
> their authority reaches will be fearful of overstepping it.
> Fix: Clarify the scope of employees' authority. With
> "specific freedom to act," employees can make decisions
> without worrying about going too far.

Policies, Procedures and Rules

Are you one of those organizations that have a rule for

everything? Do you have a policy on policies? If so, you will

need to back away from the giant three ring binders.

Some levels of policy and procedures are necessary to

ensure operational effectiveness and efficiency. Most become policy and procedure for the sake of policy and procedure. Take a critical look at your procedures, or better yet, have a group of team members take that look and determine what are needed, what can be eliminated, and what can be dramatically loosened.

At one organization in which we worked within the past five years; we encouraged the implementation of a quarterly procedural review. In the first quarter alone, a full third of the procedures were eliminated. After a year and a half of operation, the procedural review found seventy-five percent of the procedures were cumbersome, unneeded, or redundant. The result was a much more highly engaged and thinking working environment. No more dependence on procedure, but rather dependence on thinking and invested team members. Side benefits included an increase in innovative processes and higher service to customers.

To tie this to an earlier subject, if you hire bright people, you must put them in a system that allows them to be bright.

The over-reliance on policies and procedures will turn your bright team members into template punching robots. No sense to think or use judgment when the policy and procedure covers everything. This will absolutely suck the life out of good team members.

Policies and procedures are the crutch of weak managers. It is so easy to craft a procedure that covers everything but much harder to coach, encourage, and develop team members to act with degrees of freedom and utilize good judgment skills.

Micromanagement

Micromanagement, one of the most cited terms in engagement and team satisfaction surveys, is the tendency of some managers and supervisors (notice the lack of the work leader in this sentence) to overly participate in operational level issues and in tasks or projects assigned to team members.

The cause of micromanagement is when a would-be-leader has greater comfort performing work associated with the line level as compared to the job associated with an effective leader. Communication, engagement, coaching, planning, and relationship building is difficult and foreign, so many leaders retreat to whence they came and return to the line level functions in which they were very skilled at performing.

Another root of micromanagement is the high egocentricity that a leader can do it better and faster than another team member. This cause is often shown as the leader constantly adding value to a team member project or a leader questioning the status and timing of tasks assigned to team members.

Quite simply, the cure for this engagement draining issue is that leaders must lead and stay away from the jobs, tasks, and projects assigned to others. The job of a leader is different, and they don't have to prove any level of superiority or street credibility by doing the job of a team member.

Empowerment

The catchword of the twenty-first century. You're empowered. We're empowered. I'm empowered. Let's all be empowered together. Blah, blah, blah.

Empowerment is the freedom, latitude, authority, and responsibility to perform a function without interference or approval needed from anyone. It is an autonomy of action that comes with the price of being responsible for the outcome.

Many managers talk a good game related to empowerment. They use the word. They tell people that they are empowered to act, but their actions don't necessarily match those words.

The telltale examples that are frequently seen include a need for constant updates, requested email copies, and taking over when a project needs a higher level of approval or presentation. "Since this is going to the president, I better be the one that presents this" or "Keep me in the loop" or "Copy

me on those emails so I know what is going on" are all the
cover words for fake empowerment.

Genuine empowerment is risky. Team members could
make a mistake. Team members might say the wrong thing in
front of someone. They could take a path that you did not
endorse or use previously. All of those are risk factors
associated with empowerment but not the biggest one.

The biggest perceived risk of empowerment of others is
that a leader would be asked about the status of something and
gasp; they would have to acknowledge they don't know. The
fear of saying, "I don't know, but I will find out and get back to
you shortly" is pervasive in many organizations. Some leaders
falsely fear the loss of credibility associated with not knowing.
Some are just afraid of not having all the answers and believing
somehow that is a reasonable expectation.

Team members see this false empowerment for what it
is; it is not really empowerment at all. They see that the

leader's trust is limited. They feel the tether to which they are attached. This impacts satisfaction and team member engagement.

When empowering, give it away. Give it all away. The decisions, the communication, the research. All of it. Demonstrate your trust in team members and your desire to see them grow. If limitations are absolutely needed, describe them upfront and avoid getting in the middle of it or trying to add any kind of value to their work.

Errors and Complaints

Closely related to both empowerment and micromanagement is an organization's or individual leader's reaction to a mistake or a complaint.

Many organizations treat positive news with an almost blasé type of approach. A customer compliment comes in, a note is sent, and maybe the letter is posted on a bulletin board somewhere. Ho hum.

The converse is when a complaint comes in. Then everyone's hair catches fire. There are meetings, torrents of emails, stories are practiced, and the kicker, we are teaching our team members to be fearful of complaints. That fear of complaints is the opposite of the freedom to act and the freedom to do the right thing.

Same thing occurs when there is an error. Right responses and good work will often not get much notice but make a mistake and the gates of hell fly open with activity. Again, the lesson to team members is quite clear. Do good and you won't hear much. Make a mistake and hear a lot, therefore, create the fear of mistakes. Like with complaints, this is absolutely the opposite of the desired effect of the freedom to take risks, innovate, and make progress.

Chapter 15

*F*inal Notes and Encouragement

*"Start where you are.
Use what you have. Do
what you can."*
Arthur Ashe

Creating a healthy, productive, and engaged working environment is hard work. Doable. Very doable.

To pull this off successfully, an organization must start with a strong commitment at the top. Senior leaders, directors, and board members must embrace the practices of engagement and healthy workplaces. They must model them, support them, and live them.

From there, the engagement strategies must become part of the organization's culture. This culture becomes a deeply engrained set of rituals and practices that everyone is

aware of, practices, and shares with others. That cultural

immersion will then become apparent to your customers and

other stakeholders as well.

People want to be engaged. They want to enjoy coming

to work. They want to participate and do the right thing.

They are waiting for you. Your move.

*A*bout

Tim Schneider

Tim Schneider is the CEO and lead facilitator for Aegis Learning.

As the author of ***LeadWell-The Ten Competencies of Outstanding Leadership*, Tim Schneider is a widely recognized expert in leadership development, executive coaching, and healthy organizations.**

Over the past twenty years, Tim has become one of the most sought-after trainers, coaches, speakers, and professional facilitators in the nation. Renowned for both his style and content, Tim delivers powerful messages about leadership, customer service, teamwork, communication, healthy work environments and personal success. Stylistically, he brings an unparalleled enthusiasm, passion and power to his speaking and teaching which always infects his audience. His love of teaching and speaking becomes obvious within the first few minutes of each presentation. Equally obvious is his sense of humor and desire to make each session enjoyable and fun.

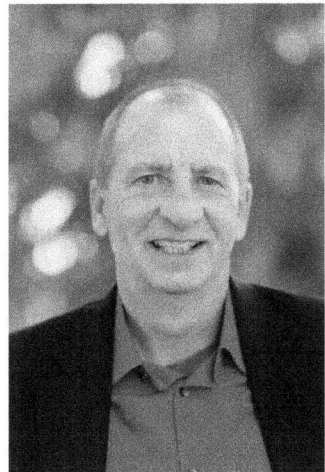

$\mathcal{R}$eferences and Footnotes

Pavlov, I. P. (1927). *Conditioned reflexes: An investigation of the physiological activity of the cerebral cortex.* Translated and Edited by G. V. Anrep. London: Oxford University Press.

Pavlov, I. P. (1927/1960). *Conditional reflexes.* New York: Dover Publications (the 1960 edition is not an unaltered republication of the 1927 translation by Oxford University Press

Kahn, William A. (1990). *Psychological conditions of personal engagement and disengagement at work.* The Academy of Management Journal, Vol. 33, No. 4 (Dec., 1990), pp. 692–724.

Gallup. (2013). *Engagement at work: Its effect on performance continues in tough economic Times.* Copyright © 2013 Gallup, Inc. All rights reserved. Gallup® and Q12® are trademarks of Gallup, Inc.

Haid, Michael and Sims, Jamie. (2009) *Employee engagement: maximizing organizational performance.* All rights reserved.

Scott, Dow, Ph.D., Loyola University and McMullen, Tom, Hay Group. (2010). *WorldatWork study of total rewards.*

The personal meaning of social values in the work of Abraham Maslow by John H. Morgan. (2012). *Interpersona: An International Journal on Personal Relationships.* ISSN 1981-6472, 06/2012, Volume 6, Issue 1, pp. 75 – 93

Maslow, A. H. (1967). A theory of metamotivation: The biological rooting of the value-life. *Journal of Humanistic Psychology.*7 (2): 93–26. doi:10.1177/002216786700700201.

Michael Daniels. *The development of the concept of self-actualization in the writings of Abraham Maslow*. University of Toronto Libraries.

Fotsch, Bill and Case, John. (2014). Share your financials to engage employees. *Harvard Business Review*. June 3, 2014

Census of Fatal Occupational Injuries, 2011. US Department of Labor, Bureau of Labor Statistics.

Riitta Hari, and Kujala, Miiamaaria V. (2009). Brain basis of human social interaction: From concepts to brain imaging. *American Physiological Review.*

Prime, Jeanine and Salib, Elizabeth. (2014). The Best leaders are humble leaders. *Harvard Business Review*

Long, Lori, PhD, SPHR. (2010). Creating flexible career paths: An employee retention strategy. Baldwin Wallace College.

Benko, Cathleen and Weisberg, Anne. (2007). Mass career customization. *Harvard Business Press.*

BaseballReference.com. Greg Maddux career statistics

Burleson, Winslow. PhD. (2005). Developing creativity, motivation, and
self-actualization with learning systems. *Journal of Human-Computer Studies.*

Heylighen, Francis, PhD. (1992). A cognitive-systemic reconstruction of
Maslow's theory of self-actualization. Free University of Brussels, Pleinlaan. *Behavioral Science Journal*

Flaherty, Colleen N. (2007). The effect of tuition reimbursement on turnover:
A case study analysis. National Bureau of Economic Research.

Rehnborg ,Sarah Jane, Ph.D., Bailey, Wanda Lee, MSW, Moore, Meg, MBA, Sinatra Christine, M.Paff. (2009). Strategic volunteer engagement: A guide for nonprofit and public sector leaders. RGK Center for Philanthropy and Community Service. The LBJ School of Public Affairs. The University of Texas at Austin

Unattributed. (2009). The benefits of employee volunteer programs, A 2009 Summary Report. JA Worldwide

Temme, J., & Katzel, J. (1995). Calling a team a team doesn't mean that it is: Successful teamwork must be a way of life. *Plant Engineering*, 49, n1. p.112(2).

DeJanasz-Dowd-Schneider. (2001*). Interpersonal skills in organization, teams in the workplace*, Chapter 15, 309-329, McGraw-Hill.

Carter, C., Bishop, J., & Kravits, S. (2007) *Keys to college studying: Becoming an active thinker. Learning styles, majors, & careers: Knowing your talents & finding your direction.*

Kreitner-Kinicki. (2003). *Organizational behavior (6th edition) group dynamics*, Chapter 12, 408-443.

Saari, Lise M. and Judge, Timothy A. (2004). Employee Attitudes and Job Satisfaction. *Human Resource Management*, Winter 2004, Vol. 43, No. 4, Pp. 395–407

Zinger, David. (2010). Avoiding employee engagement pitfalls. HRReporter

Wilson, Brady. (2014). Beyond engagement strategy #2: Minimize surveys; maximize energy-checks. Juice Blog

Taggart, Jim. (2013). Employee engagement surveys: Junk science or useful tool? Changing Winds.

Gibbs, Roydon. (2014). The risk of employee engagement surveys. The Engagement Activist.

MacLeod, David and Clarke, Nita. Engaging for success: enhancing performance through employee engagement. McLeod Report for Government.

Accenture. (2006). The high performance workforce study 2006, Executive Summary.

Axtell, C. M., Harrington, E., Holman, D. J., Unsworth, K. L., Wall, T. D. and Waterson, P. E. (2000). Shopfloor innovation: facilitating the suggestion and implementation of ideas, *Journal of Occupational and Organisational Psychology*, 73.

Corporate Leadership Council. (2004). Engaging the workforce – focusing on critical
leverage points to drive employee engagement, Corporate Executive Board.

Forth, J., Bewley, H., Bryson, A. (2006). Small and medium-sized enterprises: Findings from the 2004 workplace employment relations survey.

Garrow, V. (2008). Staff engagement: summary literature review, *Institute for Employment Studies.*

Hay Group (2008) The frustrated employee: Help me help you.

Herzberg, F. (2002) One more time – how do you motivate employees? *Harvard Business Review.*

Neugebauer, J. (2008). Best practice guide to employee engagement – hitting the right
note, Osney Media.

Coca-Cola, Inc. (2014). Our Workplace www.cocacola.com

Markey, Rob. (2014). The four secrets to employee engagement. *Harvard Business Review*

Buckingham, Marcus and Coffman, Curt. (1999). *First break all the rules*. Simon & Schuster Publishing.

Schmitt, Jeff. (2013). 12 ways to be the leader everyone wants to work for. *Forbes.*

Bischoff SJ, DeTienne KB, Quick B. (1999). Effects of ethics stress on employee burnout and fatigue: An empirical investigation. *J Health Hum Serv Admin.* 1999;21:512–32. Research Notes, Healthcare Executive 1998; November/December.

1999 National Business Ethics Study, Walker Information in association with the Hudson Institute; September 1999.

Shklover, Gene (October, 2013). Ethics and engagement. *Thinking Integral Magazine.*

Ethics Resource Center and the Hay Group (2009). Ethics and employee engagement; an empirical study and report.

Bennis, Warren; Goleman, Daniel and O'Toole, Jim. (2008). Transparency: creating a culture of candor. Wiley, John & Sons, Incorporated

TINYpulse. (2014). *7 Vital trends disrupting today's workplace.*

www.ingramcontent.com/pod-product-compliance
Lightning Source LLC
Chambersburg PA
CBHW030934220326
41521CB00040B/2320